Cover photograph: Beneath the Hirli ridge approaching zig zag path to huts.

MATTERHORN VISION

by

Brian Bonner

PUBLISHED WOODGATE PRESS

1993

British Library Cataloguing in Publication Data
(A catalogue record for this book is available from
the British Library)

Published 1990
Reprinted and Revised 1991
Reprinted and Revised 1993

Printed by
Clifford Ward & Co. (Bridlington) Ltd.
55 West Street, Bridlington, East Yorkshire
YO15 3DZ

ISBN 0 9515962 2 5

DEDICATED TO

My wife Leita who was always there with help
and encouragement and
Ivo Perren my Mountain Guide who made it all possible

ACKNOWLEDGEMENTS

My grateful thanks to the following:-

Mrs June Daw for her help in producing copies of my manuscript.

The Reverend Derek Hall, former Vicar of the Holy Trinity the Parish Church of the Langdales, for permission to quote from his audio visual colour slide show 'BETWEEN HEAVEN AND EARTH'

Hodder & Stoughton for allowing me to use a passage from Frank S. Smythe's 'AGAIN SWITZERLAND'

Mr. Beat H. Perren for permission to use his photographs as indicated

The author also gives his thanks to Photo A. Perren-Barberini for use of their photograph as indicated

CONTENTS

LIST OF ILLUSTRATIONS

PREFACE

Have you looked at the Matterhorn, or just a photograph of this soaring mountain, and sensed a fleeting mad wish that YOU would like to stand on the summit? I can remember that my courtship, or was it a feud? started in 1950 during my first visit to Zermatt. It was early spring with snow still slowly receding from the lower alpine slopes revealing a mass of delicate white and violet spring crocuses, with the Matterhorn resplendent in a full cloak of snow. As I walked up a little used path above Winkelmatten, long since developed into a rash of apartments, I remember talking to a strong impressive looking man tending his garden who surprised me with his fluent English. It turned out that he was one of the elite Zermatt Guides, and in reply to my questioning he admitted climbing the Matterhorn over 100 times, (now the Matterhorn's popularity is so great it is not uncommon for a guide to have climbed it over 300 occasions). This chance meeting sowed the seed, but it was after many more visits to Zermatt before I seriously asked myself whether I could attempt to reach the summit.

For years I nursed my secret ambition to climb the Matterhorn, but it was not until 1965 that I mentioned my thoughts to my wife Leita. Admittedly it took her some time to digest my pronouncement but from that moment the venture became a joint one. I had never done any mountaineering — fell walking, yes, but 'pitches', 'belay', 'crampons', all referred to a sport of which I knew nothing. Well meaning friends and relatives made me question the wisdom of my decision. What were the chances of success, would I strain my heart, had I a head for heights, would the cost be prohibitive? What would happen to my family if I was killed? I was then aged 42 surely it was just a question of a few months dedicated training culminating in a successful ascent? Had I known then that it would take 15 years for me to achieve success I would certainly have considered it most unlikely, that approaching 60 and used to a sedentary occupation, I would be able to take on such a challenge. Lastly, and possibly the most intriguing question of all was, why did I wish to climb the Matterhorn? As you read on I will try to answer these questions so that if YOU have asked yourself similar questions and had similar doubts it seems that we have much in common.

Most of the mountaineering books I have read are written by experts. Many of these experts are now international celebrities because of their courageous achievements. I have enjoyed their graphic accounts of physical endurance, of summits climbed, and mourned with them at tragedies suffered BUT I have always felt that I was reading a book written by someone who was superior and different from myself. I cannot compete with such heroes, indeed I blush with shame when I think of the occasions Ivo Perren, my Zermatt Guide, has shouted at my stupidity. Oh yes, these embarrassing moments will all be revealed.

9

Over the last two decades I like to think that, compared to the Frank S. Smythe era there is now a more tolerant view taken of inexperienced tourists wishing to climb the Matterhorn. Although admiring the late Frank S. Smythe for his excellent books I must admit that the following extract from his book *Again Switzerland* made me frown:-

> The task of conducting inexperienced tourists over peaks, passes and glaciers is liable to have a debilitating, even souring effect on the Alpine Guide. And small wonder. It is said that the tariff for the Matterhorn is disproportionate to that of neighbouring peaks, having regard to the fact that the ascent by the Zermatt route is comparatively easy; but the guides who throughout the season drag tourists of all shapes, sizes and descriptions up that mountain earn every centime of their pay; indeed the fatigue, both mental and physical, that they undergo is worth far more than a modest 200 fcs. Anyone interested to learn how much, should spend 12 hours of a single day lifting and raising a hundred-weight sack of coal up and down a step-ladder.'

No way, other than in an emergency, will a guide carry his client. Before he did that he would turn back since it would not be safe to continue with someone unable to climb by his own efforts. Admittedly someone may wish to achieve a life long ambition to climb a certain mountain which is way above his physical ability, then most likely he would employ a guide and a porter — one to pull, the other to push! Whatever is arranged you may be sure the professional guide will ensure there is an adequate safety margin. If a life long ambition can be achieved in this way I say 'so be it and the best of luck'. I would certainly not decry such an achievement if planned sensibly. I am thinking particularly of an ascent of the Matterhorn in 1979, by an American who had suffered several heart attacks. I think he employed a guide and a porter who took him to the Solvay Hut the first day, and continued to the summit the next day. His descent was by helicopter. This of course was an exceptional climb and certainly shows to what lengths those *obsessed* by the Matterhorn will go just to stand on the summit. I should add that generally the Zermatt guides only use the Solvay Hut in an emergency, and not as an overnight refuge. However it is comforting to know that help can be summoned from the Solvay Hut in case of need.

I was born in East Finchley, London, and educated at what was then known as Tollington Grammar School where I managed to survive somewhere at the bottom of the 'B' stream until September 1939. At that time I was on holiday in Bournemouth with my parents, who considered it wise to remain there to avoid the air raids that were expected on London. By the time we returned to London I was pleased to find that all the school had been evacuated so I had a perfect 'alibi' for not obtaining the equivalent of 'O' levels! I was fortunate to enlist as a temporary clerk with a well known national company until I was summoned for a medical examination in Leeds for H.M. Forces. As I had always considered myself to be an athlete I was shocked to be graded 4 (it seems my heart is in the wrong place), and although I appealed and was granted a second medical at Bradford the decision was the same. Because of my medical grading it was only with difficulty that I was able to join the ranks of my Company's permanent staff.

As you can imagine doubts over my physical fitness have always been with me and here is, I think, one of the reasons I felt compelled to take on the Matterhorn challenge.

As I do not wish to be *typed* so early in my narrative I will not reveal, until later, my occupation; all I will say is that I worked for $43\frac{1}{2}$ years finding solace among the Yorkshire fells and Lakeland mountains. In addition over this period I must have visited the Swiss Alps approximately twenty-one times during my annual holidays.

So much for my past. Now I have retired and my principal hobby is colour slide presentations including, of course, my *Matterhorn Story*. As I researched this subject I was struck by the fact that among the many books about climbing there was not one written by A BEGINNER FOR A BEGINNER.

I hope this book will give encouragement and advice to all who love mountains, and in particular to those who may **consider** climbing the Matterhorn. I have deliberately used the word *consider* since far too many lives (average 10-12 per year) are lost on the Matterhorn because the victims failed to calculate all the risks involved.

CHAPTER I

AN OBSESSION

This chapter has become the most difficult one to write in the entire book.

It is likely that you are asking yourself 'what makes this chap tick?' To climb the Matterhorn I had to be motiviated so I will try to explain to you how this happened.

My Concise Oxford Dictionary describes OBSESSION as 'unreasonably persistent idea in the mind'. Yes, that just about sums it up. I just could not get the idea of standing on the summit of the Matterhorn out of my mind.

How did I become obsessed? Whether you love a beautiful woman or a mountain, (hardly comparable I agree) you perceive a vision which your mind slowly but surely takes over. Yes, just like that!

One evening, after a long walk to the Schönbiel Hut and back, I sat on our balcony enjoying a satisfying drink 'topping up' my dehydrated body. As I sat I gazed, as I always did at such times, but on this occasion I jotted down what my vision was all about:- There it was, the Matterhorn, with a girdle of white cumulus cloud straddling its neck just above the Solvay Hut. The late evening sunlight emphasised the wispish choker vainly trying to throttle the Giant. I glanced up at my watch; it was 19.20hrs. and the clouds now banked up in Italy, silhouetting the jagged Zmutt ridge. Then, within two minutes, the clouds made a major assault and encircled the whole mountain, yet the summit continued to rebuff the fluffy hordes. On the East face, away from the setting sun, the clouds had become sullen and thick, yet over the Hornli ridge on the upper North face the clouds still whirled and tumbled like frothy whipped cream. Now the noose was tightened, imperceptibly the shoulders and neck of the Giant were smothered with only the top 200ft. of the final snow slope visible — within seconds this would go — or would it? Suddenly the summit burst back for a momentary gasp, and then succumbed to the clouds. The veiling of the Matterhorn took exactly 20 minutes.

But wait, suddenly it seemed as if the Giant might have the last laugh for there etherially in the clouds the summit was sensed rather than seen. It was just as if our mighty Giant was asking for a respite, a reprieve, but he knew that he was running out of time, and his plea would surely fail as the Church bells in Zermatt rang out for evening Mass.

I have been bold enough to try and describe just one evening scene. Every evening, indeed every hour, can be different, and when visible the mountain may weave its spell over you. If this happens you could, as I did, see yourself standing on the summit. Could such a vision become a reality? Only you will know the answer.

Although I have attempted to build up a word picture illustrating my motivation, I hesitate to elaborate on my religious beliefs which are never far below the surface when thinking of the Matterhorn.

In 1979, whilst on the Cima di Jassi, I met and made friends with the Rev. Derek Hall and his wife Peggy. At that time Derek was acting Pastor at the Protestant Church in Zermatt known as St. Peters the Alpine Club Church —built in 1870. Anxious to summon up all possible help to achieve my ambition I asked him, quite seriously, to remember me in his prayers. Because of an accident, I failed to reach the summit that year BUT I did return safely, and I like to think that Derek's prayers were duly noted. The Matterhorn to Derek is not only an obsession, but a symbol of life and death. I would like to quote extracts of a preface to an audio visual colour slide show given by Derek entitled *Between Heaven & Earth* as Derek can, so much more ably than I, put his religious thoughts on paper:-

"ABOUT THE FILM — BETWEEN HEAVEN & EARTH is not primarily a travel film. It is, amongst other things, meant to convey a meaning — a philosophy of life. Mountains breed mental reflections in the climber and mountain wanderer alike. Times spent in the Alps (or even our hills at home) occasionally give glimpses of ultimate truth — about God, oneself and life in general. F.W. Bourdillon, writing in the Alpine Journal says 'We have all of us had our moments', either on the mountains, or perhaps in some distant view of them, when life and joy have assumed new meanings, and the world's horizons suddenly break down and show us realms of dream — beyond and yet beyond. 'BETWEEN HEAVEN & EARTH' seeks to express in photographs and music some of those *moments* which have been felt whilst in the Alps.

The most important theme of the film is Death & Resurrection. Blatantly subjective it may be, but to us the Matterhorn is a symbol of both these themes. The former, one cannot help associating with the Matterhorn since so many have come to Zermatt to climb this mountain with tragic consequences. If the Matterhorn is a symbol of death, it is also (to us at least) a symbol of Resurrection. Like a great finger it points skywards and directs the thoughts to something which transcends life here. It stands, so to speak, as a monument to the restlessness of the spirit in man which reaches upwards for an identity and a fulfilment in something above himself". I agree.

CHAPTER 2

GUIDES

I do feel that a book dedicated to a Zermatt Guide should contain a chapter giving the reader some background information. However this is easier said than done — particularly if you are not in Zermatt — since I have found the guides to be a taciturn lot. Perhaps, in my case, this is just as well as I would rather not know what they think about my climbing.

Obviously if I could speak German fluently I would be able to converse more with my guides and find out what it is that makes a man risk his life each time he takes a climber up a mountain. Believe me this is no exaggerated statement, just you take a quick look at your Holiday Insurance Policy — look at the exclusions in small type:- I will quote — "The Insurers shall not be liable in respect of death, bodily injury by any insured person whilst taking part in mountain or rock climbing necessitating the use of ropes or guides......" so there you are! British Insurers are a clever lot, their decisions are based on proven statistics. Insurance is essential and mountaineering insurance application forms can be obtained from the British Mountaineering Council (B.M.C.) — see address in glossary.

In Zermatt a mountain guide has a season limited to July, August and September. Even during the limited summer months there are many days when the weather prohibits climbing and he earns nothing consequently, unless he has another source of income, perhaps a business or rentals from apartments, it is difficult to be financially secure. As there is no pension fund, the Guides' Association has a Retirement Fund to help support former guides in need of assistance. Moneys received from the sale of the Matterhorn Climbers Certificate (S Fr 12) and the Badge (S Fr 8) go to this fund.

Visitors have been able to hire guides for mountain tours for over a century. Here I think is one reason why guides take up their profession — heritage. To appreciate the proud heritage of the Zermatt Guides, buy a booklet from the Zermatt Museum entitled *Das Goldene Buch Der Bergführer* which lists all the principal mountains of the Valais area, recording the heights, and stating when and by whom all the alternative routes up a mountain were climbed.

The earliest recorded climb in this book dates back to 1792 but mountaineering did not become popular until the mid 19th century.

In the mid 19th century mountain dwellers scraped a living as chamois hunters, collectors of rock crystals — much used at that time in jewellery — or as peasants. I have never been happy labelling anyone a peasant since sometimes in Britain the term is stupidly used in a derogatory way, after all agriculture has always been a noble and essential way of earning a living. These occupations fitted them ideally to act as guides for the adventurous tourist. To fully appreciate the exploits of the earliest guides just compare the equipment used in those days with that used today.

At present to become a certified Mountain guide an applicant must be a good skier and climber, able to speak two languages, and possess more than his share of intelligence and brawn. This does not mean that he has to be a big man; indeed I have noticed that the majority have comparatively slight bodies and can be described as *wiry*.

Even before an applicant can become an Apprentice he has to undergo extensive courses on avalanches and snow conditions culminating in an examination he must pass. Once the Apprentice is accepted he has to undertake two further courses lasting two weeks each. The first, taken in the Spring, covers climbing on skis with descents over unknown snow pistes (i.e. tracks). The second course later in August/September concentrates on rock and ice climbing, and teaches the Apprentice how to deal with emergencies and apply basic first aid. After each course the Apprentice must pass an examination otherwise he is not allowed to proceed. After passing these four courses that have taken six weeks the Apprentice becomes an ASPIRANT. As an Aspirant he is permitted during the following year to undertake mountain excursions with Tourists BUT ONLY under the supervision of a certificated guide. During this period as an Aspirant he must **successfully** complete two final courses lasting 2½ weeks each. At last after successfully completing five courses covering 11 weeks' tuition he obtains the prized Diploma of a Swiss Mountain Guide.

A few Mountain Guides are also Ski Instructors, but this entails tuition in a different set of courses to qualify for a separate Diploma.

No guide will knowingly commence a climb with his client if he thinks the weather will create an unacceptable hazard, however sudden changes in the weather can turn a simple route into a dangerous climb. Be honest with yourself, are you as fit as your guide thinks? Are you acclimatized? Ask your guide about the weather prospects then, if you have any doubts you must make the decision whether to go.

Each night in Zermatt I try to telephone my good friend Arthur Hotz in Lucern as I know that he is watching the weather forecast on my behalf. I suggest that anybody in Zermatt planning to climb the Matterhorn should listen carefully to the short term and long term forecasts — this can save a lot of disappointment and money!

Remember a NOVICE must have good weather AND a patient Guide.

The Swiss Authorities are very concerned at the number of climbing accidents that occur each year particularly to those climbing on their own. The following advice was included in an article on mountaineering issued by the Swiss National Tourist Office:

MOUNTAIN GUIDE

The Swiss Mountain Guides are men engaged in a serious and highly responsible profession. The accidents which occur year after year to parties climbing without guides are sufficient evidence of this. A guide's first duty is to guard the safety of his clients. He is constantly concerned with the welfare and comfort of those in his care. He is required to be extremely conscientious in the exercise of this profession and he can be held legally responsible for negligence and gross errors. This is reason enough for letting him decide the route, any necessary changes in the itinerary or even a return to the starting point —

however disappointing the latter might be. He will refrain from any break-neck acrobatics and he will avoid storms, rockslides and avalanches as far as humanly possible. Details of the fees, as approved by the Government, are obtainable from the official Tourist Offices of the Mountain resorts in Switzerland (International) Reply Paid Coupons obtainable at any British Post Office should be enclosed.

At no time is it worthwhile making a financial saving and narrowing the safety factor. The Guides' Office in Zermatt will give advice on any aspect of mountaineering, and stresses that climbing the Matterhorn must be taken seriously. Even for the experienced climber hiring a guide is recommended. I would add the guides have no need to *whip* up custom since during the season there are always would be clients seeking guides. Indeed if the weather is good, particularly after a bad period, you will find it very difficult to find a guide who is free, so allow yourself sufficient time to overcome this problem. If your time is limited try to contact a guide in advance of your visit. Unfortunately this is easier said than done because unless you are in Zermatt, or know someone who can introduce you to a guide, you will find it very difficult to make any arrangements in advance.

In 1944 the British Mountaineering Council (B.M.C.) was founded, and became the representative body for all who take part in mountaineering activities in the U.K.

Between 1946 and 1948 the B.M.C. formulated a programme for the training of guides, then later in 1975 the British Association of Mountain Guides was formed. (B.A.M.G.).

The B.A.M.G. is affiliated to the 'Union International des Associations de Guide de Montagne' (U.I.A.G.M.), the International Union of Mountain Guides. The high standards, governing entry into the B.A.M.G. and U.I.A.G.M., ensure that a fully qualified guide can work abroad and command the respect traditionally held by guides from Alpine Countries.

A list of British Guides certified by the B.A.M.G. can be obtained from the address listed in the Glossary.

For 1993 the recommended rates for hiring a guide in the U.K. are:-

U.K. activities	£ 80 per day
Alpine activities	£120*
Plus agreed expenses	

*With regard to specific objectives like the Matterhorn the same rates and conditions are charged as quoted by the local Mountain Guides Office.

View from the Platthorn 3345m (10,978ft.) towards Mettelhorn 3406m (11,178ft.).

CHAPTER 3

FITNESS

If you are thinking of climbing mountains it must mean that you consider yourself able to undertake vigorous exercise. Just the same I suggest that a physical check up by your own doctor is a sensible precaution. Each time I have paid my doctor a visit he seems particularly interested in my blood pressure and heart.

When I asked the Doctor whether he thought I was foolish to attempt a climb at high altitude his answer was always the same, 'You should be alright provided you do not overdo things'. You have to decide when you might overdo things physically. If you are with a guide, this is about the only decision you have to make yourself. No one likes to take a decision to turn back before attaining any summit, but your body may revolt because you are cold, or you have a serious shortage of breath, or your legs begin to falter. You may have an insufferable headache and perhaps feel sick — all these signs must be heeded otherwise the outcome could be fatal. Yes it needs courage to retreat as well as to go on.

Good, the doctor has given the go ahead, so assuming you normally lead an active life begin training seriously three to four months before you expect to visit the Alps. It is difficult to give specific advice as no two people re-act the same way. Obviously the legs, lungs, and arms must slowly become used to increasing stress. To begin with, any exercise that increases the heart beat is beneficial. I started by jogging half a mile each morning before breakfast, increasing this to a mile after a couple of weeks. This used to increase my heart beat rate and make me perspire enough to make a shower most welcome, and I must say this routine gave me a sense of *well being* when confined to my office desk. I found a continual jog put too great a strain on my calf muscles (perhaps I wore the wrong type of shoe) so my jog turned into a quick walk between every 4th and 5th lamp post. Jogging is not my favourite exercise since when jogging only one month prior to my successful climb in 1980 I suffered severe cramp in my left calf muscle, and this almost cost me the climb at the last steep pitch leading to the final steep snow slope. I will elaborate on this problem later.

An exercise I use to strengthen my legs is climbing up and down from a kitchen chair carrying a weighted rucksack. This quickly increases the heart rate, but do not overdo this exercise, stop at any sign of undue stress such as breathlessness, dizziness, or excessive muscular pain. A degree of discomfort is necessary but a strained muscle can ruin your training schedule.

Another useful exercise that can be done without any elaborate preparation is simply the knees bend and straighten routine, working up to between 100 and 120 continuous ups and downs. This exercise does become very monotonous so I used to watch T.V. as I was performing. However be careful with this exercise. The knee is a very complex part of the leg, and I have

18

read that when bending down the thigh should **not** slope back towards the floor as this can strain the knee.

The well known *press up* exercise should strengthen the arms. I never managed more than seven to eight at a time as my right arm is particularly weak due to an accident many years ago. Just imagine climbing the Matterhorn with one arm! or even no legs! Ivo was pleased to take a climber up with one arm, and Norman Croucher, the legless mountaineer, has also reached the summit. These achievements certainly *cut one down to size.*

In addition to the above mentioned exercises that should be persevered with over a period, I suggest you finish with a few deep breathing exercises. Not only will deep breathing help to compose you after your exertions but you will, imperceptibly perhaps, increase your lung capacity at the same time.

Listen to your colleagues breathing after they have climbed some steps with you, or walked briskly up hill, the chances are they will be breathing heavily with short shallow gasps. If you also suffer in this way you will most likely have acclimatization problems at 3,000m, never mind 4,000m. I admit I do not understand the biological changes required to become acclimatized but I think that this wonderful body of ours, when faced with oxygen starvation, multiplies our red corpuscles so enabling our lungs to benefit from a greater oxygen intake. Deep breathing exercises will enable you to inhale the maximum amount of oxygen and enable you to enjoy your climbing. Remember Zermatt is 1,620m (5,316ft) above sea level. You notice this fact as soon as you walk from Zermatt Railway Station carrying or pushing your luggage up hill. When budgeting and planning your stay in Zermatt you should allow yourself a minimum of three to five days to acclimatize, and during this time make long excursions on foot, preferably above 3,000m. Indeed the higher you go the better.

Acclimatization is an unknown factor. I have spoken to a middle-aged Dutch school teacher, as we climbed the Cima di Jassi, who only arrived in Zermatt the day before and who habitually visited the higher Alps yet never suffered from it. It is quite extraordinary how just a matter of two to three hundred feet make all the difference. The effects of altitude are experienced suddenly at any height. At best it will be a bad headache accompanied by a feeling of nausea and you may be able to continue climbing, or at worst, you will be left gasping for air, unable to breathe. I have been told of an instance when this happened only three hundred feet from the Matterhorn summit —what a disappointment this must have been. If you are a smoker with aspirations to climb, then STOP SMOKING. Many, many sacrifies must be made to climb the Matterhorn and this is just the beginning!

When I asked a young medical student for information on acclimatization she kindly wrote the following list of facts. (I was particularly amused at her bracketed aside!)

(1) Rate and degree of full acclimatization improved by exercise and fitness attained below 15,000ft.

(2) Young adults acclimatize best.

Sunrise – Note Hörnli and Belvedere Huts silhouetted against snow.

Looking towards Platthorn and Matterhorn from base of Mettelhorn.

View from Wellenkuppe. 3760m. – 12,335ft.

Bronze Madonna and Child at the base of the Matterhorn.

21

(3) Possibly high carbohydrate diet helps?

(4) 50% of people have some acute symptoms if staying at or above 12,000 feet for more than 12 hours. These are:-
    (a) Headache.
    (b) Light headedness.
    (c) Irritability.
    (d) Nausea.
    (e) Vomiting.
    (f) Muscle weakness.
    (g) Difficulty in breathing.
    (h) Tiredness.

USUALLY ALL PASS AWAY SOON (THE SYMPTOMS!)

Each time I have ventured up to 4,000m I have taken with me a small bottle of dissolved Disprin or anything similar as I feel this might help alleviate a headache. Provided you are not sick and can digest the solution you should obtain some relief.

I feel that physical fitness must be allied to one's mental outlook. When you climb, each step forward needs effort and determination and you feel, unless you are totally committed that the whole exercise is bordering on the absurd. It must not be just a whim, or a passing fancy, as the Matterhorn demands dedication and effort. Those who arrive in Zermatt then climb it immediately in a pair or borrowed boots! must be few and in my opinion unfortunate. I know that success after failure is a much greater prize than success *on a plate*.

I have already mentioned the sound advice given by the Mountain Guides Office on every aspect of the Matterhorn climb. YOU MUST HEED THE ADVICE, concerning physical fitness long before arriving in Switzerland. I emphasize this fact since the guides will give priority to climbers who have tested their fitness by completing high altitude walks in Zermatt. Enjoyment of any climb is dependant on your physical condition.

CHAPTER 4

A USEFUL MORNING

After your long journey to Zermatt it is a good idea to have an easy morning. I suggest that your first *port of call* is the Information Office situated on the West side of the station Square i.e. on your right as you leave the Station heading south. As the staff at the Information Office are usually very busy, prepare a list of the questions you wish to ask:- Particulars of apartments, whereabouts of the doctors, pharmacist, heliport etc. At the same time you should buy a *Map of Hiking Trails* which gives a detailed map and description of the walks that may be done without the need of a guide. There is also a cheaper *Aerial Map* with descriptions of the same walks available for 1fc.50, and it is worthwhile having this to supplement your information.

So far so good, now stroll up the main street and admire the many splendid shops and restaurants. I am afraid that I am not an authority on the best places to eat but I have always considered that I received value for money whenever I visited the Bahnhof Restaurant or a traditional Bar/Restaurant called the Walliserstube. All Hotels and Restaurants with a mass of other useful information are listed in a booklet *Prato Borni* available free from the Information Office.

After a leisurely stroll of four or five minutes — assuming of course that you have not been tempted into any shops — you will see on your left a Pharmacist indicated by a green cross on a white background (Apotheke International) where you can enrol for 30 fcs as a member of the SCHWEIZERISCHE RETTUNGSFLUGWACHT the Air Rescue Service which is represented in Zermatt by 'AIR ZERMATT'. This private Helicopter Company operates from a Heliport situated at the North end of Zermatt, and it is difficult to imagine life in Zermatt before the use of helicopters The principal work undertaken by helicopters is the supplying of mountain huts with food and fuel.

When I first visited Zermatt mules were used for this job, now helicopters ferry heavy loads of building materials to construction sites situated in inaccessible places, plus of course undertaking mountain rescue missions. The pilots can only be described as *super men* particularly when on a rescue flight — first identifying the whereabouts of the victim, then hovering, often in dangerous winds with the rotor arm within inches of a rock face, whilst a colleague is lowered on a rope to effect the rescue. You could be the victim and as you can calculate, it would be a very costly matter for you to pick up the bill once you were safely back — that is why I recommend you pay the modest 30Fcs membership fee particularly if your insurance excludes mountaineering accidents. One of the conditions mentioned by the Association of Zermatt Guides is insurance cover for mountain rescue.

Climbers on the Untere Moseley-Platte (lower Moseley rocks) approaching the Solvay hut.
Photo: Beat H. Perren.

After passing the Pharmacist you will see on your left Wega's Book & Gift Shop then a little further on your right is the BERGFÜHRER OFFICE always in the charge of a knowledgeable guide with a lifetime's experience of his local mountains. This guide holds the key to a successful climb. At your first meeting you have to convince him of your fitness and climbing ability. He will ask you what climbs you have recently completed from Zermatt, how long you took, and whether you experienced any acclimatization problems. Yes it is rather like applying for a new job and having to substantiate your qualifications!

It is easier to engage a guide early in the Summer Season than in August; or if August has been a bad month, early September. However it is difficult to calculate exactly when the season starts since everything depends on the snow conditions. A severe winter followed by a cold spring, as in 1980, may delay the opening of the Belvedere Hut for two to three weeks leaving little time in July for climbing the Matterhorn. As a contrast in 1979 a good June and July enabled the guides to start taking their clients up at the very end of June. The weather is a most important factor so you are indeed fortunate if your precious annual holiday coincides with a fine spell in July as it is then that a novice is most likely to find a guide available. At other times guides are difficult to find because many are hired directly by clients who perhaps climb with the same guide each year often at the same time. Yes it can become the typical *Egg or Chicken first*? situation. If you are sure of your holiday dates it would be a good idea some weeks before setting off for Zermatt to write to the Guides Office for advice. You may be fortunate and be given the address of a mountain guide so you could try to arrange a training climb on the Riffelhorn, I think it is best if you arrive in Zermatt early in the season before the Guides are busy. As a novice, you will be asked to prove your ability, so it is best to arrange this training climb either before you arrive or as soon as possible on arrival. Once you are climbing with a guide you can then discuss with him your hopes and ambitions.

Be warned when visiting the Bergführer Office to allow yourself plenty of time because there is usually a queue of climbers waiting their turn for attention. I, like most English, suffer from an inferiority complex as I cannot speak a foreign language. I always admire the way the elderly guide deals patiently with numerous questions put to him in German, French, Italian and English. *Now surely* I have said to myself as I wait behind the climber receiving attention *there can be nothing more to say*? At last I catch the eye of the guide and it is my turn — I am just about to ask my question when the wretched telephone rings! Why of why do telephones have priority? Whether at the Railway Station, Tax Office etc. and now the Guides' Office I always have to stand back whilst an unknown telephone caller jumps the queue.

Should you visit the Guides' Office in the evening the chances are you will be observed not only by the guide in charge but by other guides who may be in the vicinity — either in the office or sitting on the wall opposite. Mark my words this first meeting in the Bergführer Office is crucial. In 1966 and 1971, apart from serving a 3 hour apprenticeship on the Riffelhorn, I had no trouble in finding a guide BUT 8 years later with more lines on my face and less hair it was a different story. In my own mind I am sure I unwittingly made a blunder one wet evening in July 1979. It had become a habit to call into the Guides' Office to ask whether a guide had been found who was willing to take me up the Matterhorn. On this occasion I was dressed in a lounge suit, wearing a tie and actually carrying an umbrella!!! Mein Gott or possibly il mio Dio, I can imagine onlookers thinking *What has walked into this sanctum of mountaineering? How can this man, obviously an Englishman used to the soft life, climb our Matterhorn?* Each time thereafter when I called I was advised to do yet another training climb OR the Matterhorn was considered too icy — I think that I would still be waiting now for Emil Kronig (Guide in charge) to find a guide had not Ivo Perren providentially walked into the Bergführer's Office that Sunday morning on the 15th July 1979. Actually Ivo was asked to confirm Emil's observation that the Matterhorn was too icy for me to make a successful attempt. As it was, Ivo questioned me on my experience, and on what climbs I had done during my current stay in Zermatt, and then I could hardly believe my good fortune as Ivo agreed to take me to the Belvedere Hut that afternoon and attempt the climb the next day — Monday. As you can well imagine I will be eternally grateful to Ivo, because with him I have experienced excitement, tragedy, tiredness, and mountain scenery that formerly had only been described in books written by *acknowledged* experts.

If you have time before lunch do make a visit to the Museum just a three minute walk from the Guides' Office where you can visualise what it was like over 100 years ago. Poor equipment, no Belvedere Hut, no fixed ropes but at least there were dedicated Guides. Do make this pilgrimage after all you hope to achieve the same ambition as Edward Whymper.

On the 14th July 1865 a party of Swiss Guides and English climbers, organised by Edward Whymper, were the first to reach the summit of the Matterhorn. On the tragic descent there were four fatalities. Edward Whymper's epic climb is now part of mountaineering history.

CHAPTER 5

SUGGESTED WALKS & ACCLIMATISATION CLIMBS

Following your *useful morning* I suggest you study your newly acquired maps and decide on your training timetable. If you can only spend a week in Zermatt you should first pray for good weather and then get cracking. Much will depend on your age and physical fitness as to how hard you can drive yourself. Although the walks I am about to describe are spread out over 7 days I advise you to spread the walks over a longer period. By so doing your less energetic partner (?) will be able to enjoy your company on your so called *rest* days.

DAY 1 RIED — TUFTERN — SUNNEGA — FINDELN

Assuming you have never climbed a rock face I suggest you pop back smartly to the Guides' Office and try to arrange a visit this very afternoon to the Riffelhorn with a Guide to make sure you have a head for heights. Most likely you will have to wait until tomorrow so if your afternoon is free limber up by walking via Ried and Tuftern to Sunnega then return via Findeln. Consult your maps and numerous path signs dotted all over Zermatt. Remember the signs show the average time it takes to walk to your destination, and so long as you are not tempted into what Leita and I jokingly call *Franc Traps* for refreshment you will complete the journey well within the time stated. Often you have a choice of routes so obviously the less time it takes, the steeper the ascent. As a keen photographer I found it most frustrating having to walk against the clock as the views, the alpine flowers, not to mention those so called *Franc Traps* all tempt you but, as *fitness* is your aim, try to press on.

If your holiday includes a partner not obsessed with the desire to climb the Matterhorn then tact and consideration are essential! Suggest, perhaps, that you will wait at the top and he/she can take the longer zig-zag. While you are waiting, put your sweater on, and if you are truly dedicated find a quiet spot to do some of those exercises you practiced at home. As you walk through the trees, time and time again you obtain magnificent views of the Matterhorn, of Zermatt, and the mass of exciting peaks to the west. Having reached Sunnega your partner, assuming you have one, may prefer to descend by the Sunnega Bahn, but do snatch a few minutes to watch the antics of the marmots as they emerge from their burrows situated below the Sunnega Restaurant — just below the broad path that takes the long sweep down to Findeln. There are not as many of these little creatures at this particular spot as there were before the Sunnega Bahn was built. Possibly the noise and vibrations made by drilling through the rock when building the railway scared some marmots away to other burrows — perhaps they will soon return.

Findeln can be reached by a direct but steep path leading from the small plateau outside the Sunnega Station, or as mentioned by the broad path below the Restaurant. I prefer the latter route as you obtain superb views across to the Trift Valley, above which can be seen the Wellenkuppe and Rothorn. Also if you care to clamber up the small alp on your left as you proceed, you find a lovely carpet of alpine flowers in July. At Findeln, visit the small picturesque Church and admire its superb position with our mountain dominating the backcloth. As you continue down to Zermatt you will be able to appreciate the late afternoon sunlight playing etherial tricks on the Matterhorn and adjoining glaciers. The ascent is gradual so your legs will have no problems but here it might be a good idea to sound a note of caution regarding long descents. I am thinking of my descent down the Trift Valley on my return from climbing the Platthorn, and also the long descent from the Gornegrat to Zermatt. I find that for prolonged distant descents I need a cotton elastic bandage to support my left knee, otherwise, I can end up finishing the descent like an injured crab walking backwards. Despite this weakness in my knee I was not troubled in descending the Matterhorn since a climbing descent does not put as much strain on your knees as a walking descent.

DAY 2. RIFFELHORN & GORNEGRAT

If you are sampling the Riffelhorn with a Guide today he will no doubt leave you about mid-day giving you time to walk up to the Gornegrat Hotel, or higher, if you wish to admire the most magnificent mountain panorama in Europe. Certainly walk back to Zermatt if you wish but take care of those knees.

DAY 3. THEODULE GLACIER — KLEINE MATTERHORN — BREITHORN

It is absolutely essential for you to ensure that you are fully acclimatized so I recommend a climb up the Breithorn. During the season there are sufficient tourists to make this a daily excursion planned by the Guides' Office. The cost in 1992 was 110fcs. per person plus cable car return fare 35fcs. — a reservation has to be made at the Guides' Office the night before you intend to go. However if a party of three or four can be organised to share the expense of a guide I consider it preferable to make a two day tour walking to the Gandegg Hut 3,029m. the first day. (If time is limited the hut can be reached in 20 minutes from the Trochener Steg cable car station). The Gandegg Hut is situated above the Unt. THEODULGLETSCHER and I will never forget my first glacier walk when I left the Gandegg Hut about 4.30 a.m. and roped up with my good friend Arthur G. Hotz from Lucern. Suddenly Arthur pointed up towards the Matterhorn summit. A delicate pink glow slowly but surely began creeping down the east face. To the east the sky turned from a delicate pink wash to amber, and then as the sky brightened, the dull somewhat dirty surface of the glacier reflected the rising sun. For a *Towny* i.e. someone more used to concrete and bricks than mountains, this was indeed a magical morning. There is no finer spectacle than an alpine sunrise and surely a humble tourist after climbing to a mountain hut and getting up at 4 o'clock in the morning has earned a right to call himself a mountaineer? No? Oh well perhaps not. I admit that my recollections of this first glacier walk are hazy since it was over 40 years ago but I can remember that we were unable to wash before leaving the hut as the water had frozen!

I don't think the walk up the Theodule Glacier was particularly strenuous until the final stretch up to the Plateau Rosa. As we breasted the final slope our faces were blasted with fine wind driven snow, ahead was a rope of two, bending and plodding across a streaming carpet of snow. I immediately thought of an illustration in an old book I have, depicting the journey of our national hero *Scott of the Antarctic*. At this point it was decided that Leita, because of the severe wind, should make for the Italian shelter Testa Grigia and wait for our return from the Breithorn. Arthur was the *anchor man* on the rope and we made good progress to the base of the Breithorn resisting the temptation to climb the Kleine Matterhorn on the way. We started the ascent but all was not well with Bonner. I was beginning to gasp for air and to suffer from a severe headache between the eyes. However, not to be daunted, I struggled upwards slipping on each step. Vibram soles were not worn in those days, instead I had metal studs in my boots and these had a coating of frozen snow. In addition we only possessed one ice axe which Arthur gave me but as the slope became steeper Arthur sensibly decided that we had better turn back. So I did not make the summit because I was not acclimatized and not properly equipped. In 1980 I made the Breithorn summit with a party using the Kleine Matterhorn cable car. Yes, I obtained some satisfaction but thought I had cheated by using the cable car instead of the Gandegg Hut.

DAY 4. RECCE TO HORNLI & BELVEDERE HUTS OR PREPARATION FOR MATTERHORN CLIMB

Today could be the start of your great adventure. Assuming you have been able to engage a guide you will be spending the night at the Belvedere Hut. If so, I expect you will spend the morning checking equipment, pampering your feet, and having a good lunch. You can take the cable car to the Schwarzsee at about 15.00 hrs. then walk to the Belvedere Hut. It is possible that your guide will accompany you and this is preferable to meeting him at the hut since you both then have the opportunity of getting to know each other. Sometimes your guide will not be able to accompany you as he may be climbing that day with another client, so will have to meet you later at the hut.

The walk from the Schwarzsee cable car station to the Belvedere Hut takes $1\frac{1}{2}$ hours -2 hours if you are pushing it so you should arrive about 17.30 hrs. or 18.00 hrs.

If you are not climbing the Matterhorn tomorrow, why not do a recce to the Hornli and Belvedere Huts (situated side by side). It is worth mentioning that the Hornli Hut belongs to the Swiss Alpine Club and is used mainly by experienced amateur climbers, whereas the Belvedere Hut belongs to the Zermatt Commune and is run as a commercial enterprise.

From the Roman Catholic Church in Zermatt the route to the Schwarzsee via Zum See can be walked energetically in under 2 hours, but to do this you only have time to brush the drips of perspiration from your brow. On the latter part of the walk you have impressive views across to the Gorner Glacier, Breithorn and Monte Rosa not forgetting our little friend the Riffelhorn. You will be tempted to stop for photographs but try not to spoil your walking rhythm. When the cable car station and Schwarzsee Hotel come into view you will be impressed at the sheer bulk and height of the Matterhorn. At this point I find it difficult to watch where I am going as I start imagining myself actually climbing the Hornli Ridge. No bad thing using your imagination since it helps to prepare you for the worst and then, should the actuality not be so bad, you have a bonus.

By the time you have reached the Schwarzsee you will have earned yourself the time for a snack. Find time to visit the Schwarzsee Chapel (said to have been built by a Shepherd as a thanksgiving for his safe deliverance after losing his way in a storm) before proceeding up the track towards the moraine at the bottom of the FURGG Glacier. You cross this moraine and follow the path that climbs steeply up the side of the Hirli — the moraine at this point drops away steeply to your left, and fixed to the rock face on your right is a steel cable to assist climbers when conditions may be bad, but beware of frayed wire on the cable. At one point the path has collapsed but a log bridge has been built across this difficulty.

The path now swings back on its track as it climbs steeply to the comparatively level path (see cover photograph) which you follow until the commencement of the final zig-zag path up the rampart to the two huts. Before continuing, look round. There it stands just daring you to challenge it. See the depth of the Matterhorn Glacier with layer upon layer of ice and snow. Turn your gaze to the Dent d'Herens to the south west. The Dent Blanche, Ober Gabelhorn, Wellenkuppe, Rothorn, Weisshorn to the west and north west, and Zermatt with the Visptal valley to the north. The circle of mountains continues with the Mischabel Group including the Taschhorn and Dom to the north east. Finally you come full circle (you will have to clamber up the ridge to the east for an uninterrupted view) to see the Allalinhorn, Rimpfischhorn and Strahlhorn, Cima di Jazzi, Monte Rosa, Liskamm, Breithorn and Kleine Matterhorn. The final 40 minutes up the zig-zag path should not prove difficult, but early in the season, when the path can be solid with frozen snow, the tourist with no rope or ice axe should consider joining a guided excursion arranged by the Guides' Office. You will see that ropes have been erected to prevent tragedies so be careful. As climbers can be beneath, you must tread carefully to avoid kicking down stones and rocks. This is a hazard that will be with you from here-on, so for everybody's sake take great care. Eventually after climbing about forty-three zig-zags you have time to straighten your back and look up to see the Belvedere and Hornli Huts 3,260m. The former is classified as a Hotel and its tariff is shown in the Zermatt Hotel Summer Tariff. The overnight cost for yourself and guide is approximately 80fcs. and this includes bunk, dinner and breakfast for both. I have stayed on three different occasions and been well satisfied — apart from the night when my bedmates were two stalwart Japanese climbers — one snored all night, and the other made a duet by adding noises made by another quarter of his anatomy. That sure was a long night enlivened by the said Japanese who had decided to leave very early, so at 3.00 hrs. they scuffled about, dressed and clumped downstairs only to find the entrance locked! so back they clattered for a further 1½ hours — was I pleased to get up.

So far as the Hornli Hut is concerned climbers cater for themselves, and the charge for overnight accommodation is in accordance with the tariff charged for most Swiss Alpine Club huts which is, at the present time 1990, 15 fcs. for members and 20 fcs. for non members. There are reductions for those under the age of 16.

Before descending, do climb up behind the Belvedere Hut and make your way to the starting point of the actual climb. If possible try to be there early, before the sun's rays have moved too far south, then you will see at its best a magnificent bronze Madonna and Child erected in 1983 by the Zermatt guides on a rock ledge just above the mountain base.

Should you decide to use the cable car back to Zermatt it is advisable to check the time of the last departure to Furi from the Schwarzsee cable car station on the outward journey.

It is worth mentioning that a most useful booklet entitled *Prato Borni* can be obtained free from the Information Office. This booklet is full of local information such as:- Cable car times, taxi tariffs, shop opening hours etc.

DAY 5. THE BIG CLIMB? IF NOT HOW ABOUT THE ASCENT OF THE METTELHORN?

I sincerely hope that today you achieve success. Five days preparation is a very short time, so if you are successful you can congratulate yourself and also consider that *Lady Luck* has been kind to you.

If your stay in Zermatt is longer than a week and you are still getting your lungs and limbs in shape why not have a go at the Mettelhorn 3,406m (ll,178ft). This climb is certainly a test of your stamina since Zermatt is 1,620 m. above sea level; so you will be climbing in one day 1786 m. compared with approximately 1,200 m. on the Matterhorn ascent.

Your map of hiking trails states that the Mettelhorn summit can be reached in 5 hours — you must not waste any time if this target is to be achieved. You will also see whether you are becoming acclimatized — particularly the last 500 feet as you zig-zag up to the summit.

I must admit that this mountain has, over the years, been as illusive as the Matterhorn — but not as expensive since it is not necessary to hire a guide. My first attempt on the Mettelhorn was in July 1966 but then two factors made me turn back:- Deep soft snow and a broken watch. The next attempt was in 1979 and to my annoyance and embarrassment I found, too late to rectify matters, that I had climbed the Platthorn 3345 m. However, as I recollect, the view from the Platthorn was as interesting as that from the Mettelhorn as one has a fine view of the glacial approach to the Mettelhorn and the well scoured zig-zag path to the summit. A few years back as I was driving with Norman Croucher, the indomitable legless mountaineer, I told him of my *faux pas*, he laughed and said I was in very good company as he knew of other climbers who had made

(Photo: A. Perren-Barberini)

KEY TO MATTERHORN PICTURE

1.   Hirligrat (Hirli ridge).
2.   Zig Zag path to huts — about 43 zig zags.
3.   Belvedere and Hornli huts.
4.   Bronze Madonna and Child.
5.   Hornligrat (Hornli ridge).
6.   Im Steinschlag — danger of falling stones here.
7.   Eseltritte (Ass's step).
8.   Alte Hutte (Old hut).
9.   Gebiss — steep rock slabs.
10.   Unterer Moseley Platte (Lower Moseley rocks).
11.   Solvay Hut at 4003 m. (13,133 ft.).
12.   Oberer Moseley Platte (Upper Moseley rocks).
13.   Unterer Roter Turm (Lower Red Tower).
14.   The Shoulder.
15.   Oberer Roter Turm (Upper Red Tower).
16.   Fixed ropes on north face — where accident occurred.
17.   Fixed ropes on ridge leading to summit snow slope.
18.   Swiss summit 4477.5 m. (14,690 ft.).
19.   Italian summit 4476.4 m. (14,686 ft.).
20.   Furgg-grat (Furgg ridge).
21.   Zmuttgrat (Zmutt ridge).
22.   Nordwand (North wall).

Approximate climbing times if conditions are good and no ice:-

Ascent between 3 and 11 — 2 hours
Ascent between 11 and 18 — $2\frac{1}{2}$ hours
Total descent time say 5 hours
Likely total time on mountain 10 hours, with experienced climbers taking much less time.
Heights calculated approximately at 1 metre = 3.2808 ft.

the same mistake.

In 1985 I left my apartment at 6 a.m. well prepared — waterproofs, thick pullover cake & chocolate, compass, torch, whistle, AND TWO WATCHES! As I passed the Gornergrat Railway Station I noticed about a dozen people waiting for the train to take them up for the sunrise. The steep path up the Trift Valley starts halfway up the main street of Zermatt. To begin with you have the benefit of street lamps but these are soon left behind. The first spot I identified in the dark was the disused Ibex enclosure on my left then a little later the path twists through a Pine Forest and I had to use my torch as it was so dark. Of all the walks from Zermatt I find the beginning of this walk up the Trift Valley the most depressing, Plod, plod, plod — step after step — you never seem to get anywhere. At last, about 1 hour after leaving Zermatt the gloom lifts as you leave the trees behind and pass the Edelweiss Restaurant. By now the sun had risen, not dramatically as there were a lot of clouds. For a short distance the path levels out but soon steepens as it rises to cross over the rushing torrent of water pounding down into Zermatt from the glaciers above. About here I was overtaken by a young German couple who, I hoped, were making for the Mettelhorn since as a lone climber I always feel vulnerable. Alas when we reached the Trift Hotel, they branched left for the Hohbalmen — a magnificent walk I had done the day before. The path for the Mettelhorn takes a wide turn to the right or you can clamber up the steep Alp behind the Trift Hotel from here-on you climb steadily up through the Triftchumme. If the clouds allow, good views of the Matterhorn and Furgg ridge in the early morning sunlight can be obtained. Do not ignore the panorama over your left shoulder to the south west because the summits of the Ober Gabelhorn, Wellenkuppe, and Zinal Rothorn tower over their respective glaciers high above you. Suddenly I noticed a group of climbers who must have come from the Rothorn Hut and was amused to hear one of them, an accomplished trumpeter, give vent to their high spirits by playing a rallying call. As I anticipated when I finally caught up with them on the Mettelhorn I found they were Italians — what a cheerful friendly race they are, such a contrast to we north Europeans.

At about 9.20 a.m. the path lost all vestige of grass and rose steeply to the south base of the Platthorn. At this point the track fades, however look out for cairn markers traversing half right towards the saddle ridge ahead, behind which is the easterly spur of the Hohlicht glacier leading to the base of the Metterlhorn.

Unless there has been a recent snow fall you will see a distinct trail bearing half right from the saddle up the glacier. Without crampons I found the glacier very icy and my walking stick was a great help. As I stopped to take a photograph the summit of the Mettelhorn peeped over the snow horizon, I put my walking stick down and in a flash it skidded away fown the glacier. Luckily a Swiss family picked it up and returned it to me on the summit. Fortunately the weather was fine with other climbers around, but if you think there may be a risk of cloud descending I suggest you take compass bearings back to the ridge and to the Mettelhorn. From the base of the Mettelhorn, depending on your fitness, it should only take you some 15/20 minutes to reach the summit. The views all round you are impressive. Clockwise starting from the north, if you are fortunate, you see the peaks of the Bernese Oberland — the Mischabel group of mountains to the east, as you turn to the south Allalinhorn — Rimpfischhorn — Monte Rosa — Liskamm — the two snow humps of Castor and Pollux — Breithorn — Kleine Matterhorn — Matterhorn — finishing with the western summits of Ober Gabelhorn — Wellenkuppe — Zinalrothorn and Weisshorn.

Now comes the painful part of the climb, at least I find my left knee prefers the ascent! Before stepping once more on to the glacier admire the view across to the spiky pinnacles at the base of the Platthorn and to the Matterhorn beyond.

On the descent once you are off the glacier and across the rocky terrain bringing you once again to the sparse pastures of the Triftchumme, watch out for some elevated ground on your right (west). If you walk across this elevated plateau you can enjoy a closer look at the Glaciers and Zinal Rothorn.

When you have regained the path look out for an alternative route to Zermatt that branches left before reaching the Trift Hotel. I prefer this descent to returning down the Trift Valley because for the whole of the descent you have at least half of the panorama, described from the summit, stretched out in front of you and changing colour in the afternoon sunlight.

DAY 6. SCHÖNBIELHUTTE

Although I have merrily suggested a fresh excursion each day I admit that I intersperse the strenuous days with something less energetic with Leita. This can only be done if you are staying two weeks in which case this is an admirable excursion with which to start your training. Not too strenuous so provided your partner enjoys a long walk of some 14 miles or 22 Km. this is an outing you can enjoy together. I must stress that the walk is long and energetic but not to be compared, fatigue wise, with the Mettelhorn climb.

As with all your walks from Zermatt spend time on a little research. Decide which route to follow, and make sure that you start by following the correct sign posts since invariably there is a quick way and a slower less steep way.

For this trip you should take the road out of the village towards the Matterhorn, passing the Catholic Church and cross the bridge, over the rushing torrent, where many years ago villagers used to take their washing. As soon as you have crossed the bridge you must decide whether to take the broad mule track to Zmutt, which should take about an hour, possibly 50 minutes, or follow the sign on your right to Herbrigg, Hubel and Zmutt. This route is more demanding and will take possibly an hour longer than on the mule track but it is, I feel, better suited for the Matterhorn trainee!

Assuming you take the high route follow the stone flagged road sign-posted on your right until the route becomes a path leading you up the alp; look back and admire the view across Zermatt to the start of the Visptal valley stretching back to the north. If it is July the profusion of alpine flowers is a joy to see. Continue climbing and if it is warm and sunny you will now be vapourising all the coffee you drank at breakfast. I hope your conscience will stop you so early on the walk from gazing overlong at the Matterhorn that begins looming over you. As the climb progresses, particularly after Zmutt, you begin to see our mountain from a different angle. Slowly the Matterhorn's shape alters from a pyramid to a sprawling wave the crest of which is about to smash itself against the Dent d'Herens. Just to see the Matterhorn from the north west makes this walk to the Schönbiel Hut a day to remember. Where the path levels out, before descending to Zmutt, the alp becomes a haven for marmots so listen for their shrill cries. About here you may also come across a herd of goats — if you are tempted to feed them titbits make sure that they cannot grab any other belongings — I warn you they grab at anything!

If you are early Zmutt will be quiet, and you will be able to appreciate the wooden chalets, boxes of geraniums and the typical Swiss atmosphere. Later if it is a fine day, every chalet selling refreshments will have its quota of tourists. Your path goes to the centre of Zmutt, then follow the Schönbiel sign to the right. On each side the path is covered here and there with splendid purplish red, many rayed flowers sporting fleshy leaves which have the unusual, and I feel misplaced name of, Cob-webbed House-leek. Press on and you will see below you on your left the ugly dam, a man made lake filled with murky glacier water. Soon you arrive at a small plateau spotted here and there with large rocks giving welcome relief from the sun and inhabited by sheep ekeing out an existence on the sparse grazing land.

From the small plateau you will now be able to see a waterfall, then further on in the distance the Schönbiel Hut perched upon a grassy ridge to the right.

As you proceed admire the changing shape of the Matterhorn and Dent d'Herens, the rushing streams cutting across your path, alpine flowers and interesting geological rocks (superb examples of glacial rock formations) so time passes quickly and you are soon at the waterfall climbing up a steep crumbling rock path to the top. Now you are much nearer to the slaggy moraine of the Zmutt Glacier. In about 15-20 minutes the route divides — to the right a track ascends to the Arben Bivouac 3,200m. (10,500 ft.) and you will see the forbidding Arben Glacier disgorging its share of glacier water. Our route leads over a shallow stream, then 5 minutes on, you come to a short steep climb up a rough road presumably used by the local Water Authority. At this point the road/path from Staffelalp joins our route. Next paddle or stone hop across the shallow river (this could be difficult in wet weather) fed by the Hohwang Glacier. By now the Matterhorn is parallel with your left shoulder —just think *you* hope to get up there!

Now you are once more on dry land, the path takes you through a small rocky area, interspersed with sheltered grassy hollows where you are surrounded by alpine flowers not found lower down. If your partner suggests a breather here, why not? after all it wasn't your suggestion was it? The final 30/40 minutes of the walk remains — a short ridge walk along the crest of the moraine. If there is a strong wind blowing, your partner may need some supportive encouragement here — stress this is the last tricky bit and you will soon be congratulating each other on reaching the final zig-zag up to the hut. I was impressed by the superb position and by the solid stonework of the hut set solidly behind a spacious walled forecourt. The weather began to change on our arrival — flecks of sleet blew into our faces and we were thankful to enter the hut and enjoy a nourishing bowl of hot savoury soup costing a modest 3fcs. Forty years ago — good Lord, was it so long ago? — when we first visited this hut, we were introduced to the Valais *thirst quencher* Fendant wine and mineral water. I have never drunk anything so satisfying — although on this last occasion our soup was just as welcome.

Before returning, take a good look at the view for you are looking at one of Europe's finest panoramas. I was amazed to learn that in the year 1.11.87—31.10.88, 1,632,614 visitors were recorded as **staying** in Zermatt. Perhaps only one or two per cent of these visitors see this view from the Schönbiel Hut, so you will be one of the privileged few.

DAY 7. ANOTHER STRENUOUS WALK : ZERMATT — TUFTERN —OBERROTHORN — FLUHALP — SUNNEGA — ZERMATT

This walk will certainly test your stamina — second perhaps to the Mettelhorn but, none the less rewarding if the weather is good, as you will have an exhilarating panorama of the Mischabel group of mountains.

The first part of the walk will be familiar to you if you followed my suggestion for day 1. You start on new ground from Tuftern where you pick up the track to Täschalp then branch right through the TUFTERNKUMME to the saddle between the Unterrothorn and the Oberrothorn (refer to excursion map). From the saddle ascend the Oberrothorn. I realize this has over simplified matters as it is a very strenuous scramble to the summit, and on this walk it is prudent to have a companion. Once on the summit, be very careful if it is icy, just feast your eyes on the giants opposite:- The Täschhorn, Dom, etc. From the summit there is a narrow steep track leading down to the principal path to the Fluhalp, but if you are on your own you can retrace the route to the saddle and descend by the recommended route to the Fluhalp Hut. By the time you reach the hut you will have earned yourself a beer.

You stay at the Fluhalp Hut when you climb the Rimpfischhorn or Strahlhorn. Refreshed by your beer you now have a welcome panoramic down hill walk via the Stellisee. If there are broken clouds, admire the shafts of light shining on to the Matterhorn Glacier and glaciers to the east. By now you will have been on the go for 7-8 hours so you may be excused for feeling the odd ache and pain.

You will no doubt continue down to the Sunnega where I decided that if I was going to arrive back in time for dinner prepared by Leita, I had better use the Sunnega Bahn.

You supermen may well decide to complete the walk to Zermatt via Findeln, in which case before leaving the Fluhalp Hut consult your map and take the lower route leading to Findeln. The complete walk, allowing for breaks and photography, will take 8-10 hours.

The advantage of this excursion, apart from the superb scenery, is that your partner has the option of meeting you at a number of places *en route*. You can meet at the saddle between Unterrothorn and Oberrothorn (partner takes cable car to summit of Unterrothorn and descends to saddle), or at the Fluhalp

37

Hut. A cable car from Sunnega can be taken to Blauherd and it is just an easy stroll to the Fluhalp Hut.

Should you be so unfortunate as to have wet weather, you have my heartfelt sympathy having experienced rain more than once day after day —remember three times my plans were halted through inclement weather. If you are only staying a week, grit your teeth, put on your waterproofs, a towel round your neck, and walk regardless, after such outings that hot bath is sheer bliss. Remember just one day's heavy rain in Zermatt can mean snow and ice for days on the Matterhorn. If the clouds close in for days and your clouds of depression become too much, take a $\frac{1}{2}$ fare with your Holiday Ticket to Stresa in Italy, you might just be lucky and find the sunshine. One thing for sure you will find some cheap drink with which to drown your sorrows.

So much for my suggested excursions. Obviously there are many more walks you can plan yourself, so study your maps and take another tipple as you plan.

CHAPTER 6

FAILURES AND SUCCESS

I have said in an earlier chapter that in my opinion success after failure is a much greater prize than success on a plate.

If your holidays are limited to three or four weeks a year, you are indeed fortunate if all your plans and all your efforts are blessed with good weather during your precious holiday in Zermatt.

In 1966 I went *cap in hand* to my Personnel Officer and asked if I could take an extra week in August to climb the Matterhorn. You see I wished to enjoy two weeks seaside holiday with Leita and our young daughter Pat AND take a week off on my own in Zermatt all within the peak holiday period. To my surprise, my request was granted so I found myself walking up the main street of Zermatt the very afternoon England won the World Football Cup by beating West Germany. It was very sunny, and the street was deserted as most of the inhabitants were gathered round television sets inside the numerous restaurants and little *Stublis* — the equivalent of our country inns. Feeling very much a stranger, I peered through a window and saw on the television white shirted players, who I thought were English, and dark shirted players I assumed were German. As I watched, the white shirted players conceded a goal and I turned disappointedly away thinking that the Germans were in command. Only much later did I learn the result and found that the English on this occasion were wearing dark shirts.

The omens seemed good. I had been introduced to a good looking young guide called Gotlieb Perren, and he had agreed to take me up the Matterhorn, but first recommended a climb on the Riffelhorn with another guide —Alfred Biner. This was the first time I had met any of the Zermatt Guides and I must admit that I regarded them with some awe.

The climb on the Riffelhorn was a completely new experience. It did not take long to reach the summit, but then the excitement began. To my consternation, I was told to descend the other side — the side dropping, or so it seemed, straight down to the Gorner Glacier. I was shown how to clamber down facing outwards from the mountain, leaning forward for hand holds as we descended. It was steep, but not so steep as to make it necessary to face into the rock face. This fact surprised me as I had been told that conditions on the Riffelhorn were similar to those found on the Matterhorn. Half way down Alfred Biner belayed me and asked me to wait until he called. He then climbed a little to our left straight up a vertical rock face. I thought *now I will watch closely so that I will be able to follow without any problems.* I am sure Alfred Biner will not mind my saying that he is a big man, so I thought as I weighed less I would have no trouble. Somehow it did not work out like that. The first foot hold, or an apology for one, was a very small knob of rock polished like a marble by thousands of vibram soles. Eventually Alfred Biner called — I threw off the belay — took a deep breath — placed my right boot on the polished knob and launched myself up landing at the feet of Alfred Biner like a large fish! My arms were scratched but at least I was there and not dangling at the end of the rope. That was the climax of our climb and we climbed up to the south west buttress to descend by the easy normal route.

Alfred Biner must have reported back favourably to Gotlieb Perren as our Matterhorn climb was arranged for the coming Thursday. BUT the very day of the Riffelhorn climb the clouds closed in and it rained until the Friday when the Matterhorn emerged from the clouds with a white cloak making conditions too difficult, at least for me. As a consolation I walked up to the Belvedere Hut on the Friday and was struck by the strong physique of a young German who intended climbing the next day — Saturday — the day I had to return. As I disconsolately made for the Railway Station at 13.30 hrs. I saw the young German celebrating his successful Matterhorn climb with a circle of admiring friends at the Bahnhof Restaurant. Considering the snowy conditions he had done extremely well to have returned to Zermatt by 13.30 hrs. His happy face, as I congratulated him, was a contrast to my own thoughts. To this day I ask myself whether I should have 'phoned my boss and made an excuse to stay longer as the weather was improving. Leita thought that I should have stayed — So ended attempt Number 1.

ATTEMPT NO. 2, in 1971 never really got off the ground. We had decided on a two week family holiday in Zermatt hoping that I would have the opportunity to have another attempt at climbing the Matterhorn. We booked in at the Alpina Hotel and the plan was for me to get fit and climb during the second week. I was then only 48 and I had no difficulty in arranging to meet a Guide called Victor Imboden at the Belvedere Hut. On my walk up to the Belvedere Hut from the Schwarzsee I met a sturdy individual who was then so I thought the Manager of the Anglia Building Society at Whitehaven. I mention our meeting as he kindly sent me a transparency of himself on the Matterhorn summit which he climbed a week after our meeting. Unfortunately, we experienced a severe storm that lasted the whole night and well into the next morning. We all had to descend but the Building Society Manager stayed a week longer and the weather improved. I remember the lightning was so bad as we descended on the cable car, that the cable stretching down to Zermatt was covered with a blue oscillating flame. So ended attempt number two, without any positive achievement, except the photograph of the Building Society Manager on the summit made me more determined than ever to stand on the same spot.

As a postscript I must tell you that last August 1992 I visited Whitehaven with Leita and discovered that the Building Society Manager was Allen Walker of the Bradford & Bingley Building Society (Not Anglia B/S).

Unfortunately Allen was not at his Branch when we called but later he wrote to tell me of his splendid climb in 1971. Despite very difficult snow conditions Allen and his guide were up and down by 11.30 a.m. a very fast time indeed as crampons were used the whole time. Allen was told later that he was the only climber to have reached the summit since our earlier abortive attempt.

Climbers on Im Steinschlag. Summit overhead.

The final 100m. to the Matterhorn summit and upper roof.

41

ATTEMPT NO. 3, in 1979 is a story of high hopes followed by bad luck, frustration and disappointment. Now remember I was then aged 56 with less hair, more lines on my face, and maybe I looked frail compared with most men of the mountains.

Immediately on arrival I reported to the guide in charge at the Guides' Office and said I wished to climb the Matterhorn. I took his advice and went on long excursions each day, many of which I have already described, culminating in the climb of the Cima di Jazzi completed without any acclimatization problems. I was, in my opinion, fitter than at any time before or since. Towards the end of the first week there were two days of intermittent rain (snow on the Matterhorn) but by the middle weekend the weather improved. I have already described the difficulties Emil Kronig had in finding me a Guide, and the good fortune I had in meeting Ivo Perren that Sunday morning in July 1979. Ivo explained that as he had already arranged to climb with a client the coming Tuesday, he could only climb with me the next day i.e. Monday so this meant we had to set off for the Belvedere Hut within four hours. After fixing me up with a pair of crampons we parted having agreed to meet at the Cable Car Station at 15.00 hrs. Ivo has a good knowledge of English (language and people) and a quiet confident manner. If Ivo undertakes to guide you to the summit then only a catastrophe will stop him, provided you match his determination.

When I returned to our apartment and told Leita my news I could tell from her anxious face that she felt that this time the climb was well and truly on. We packed my rucksack, checked and re-checked all my clothing, and I tried to familiarise myself with the crampons — without much success I must add: Then we were on our way to the Cable Car Station. We arrived about the same time as Ivo and I noticed his red pullover with the markings of a Guide and Ski instructor. I introduced Ivo to Leita who quickly took a parting photograph — I am sure that Leita thought this would be the last she would see of me — at least alive.

Although it had clouded over a little, there was still plenty of blue sky and I was looking forward to the walk up to the Belvedere Hut. As you are climbing or walking up a steep slope bowed down by your haversack, your eyes instinctively pick out the next place to put your feet and your mind wanders and dwells on the problems, and sometimes joys of life. As I plodded up behind Ivo I began to imagine what lay ahead and said a silent prayer that this time my efforts would prove successful.

We did not hurry, and after about 2 hours we arrived. The hut was busy since there was a contingent of climbers from Peru under the instruction of Swiss Guides. Evidently the Peruvians were training to become mountain guides for their own tourist industry. My first task was to find a vacant bunk, all the lower bunks were already taken so I had to clamber up to a top one. I learned on this climb that if you are on the top bunk you must get organised for the night. It is certainly a nuisance having to go to the toilet during the night, so take precautions. You will not have a convenient cord to pull to put on the light, so take your torch, watch and handkerchief with you. Hm! he'll be telling us how to blow our noses next — I can sense you thinking, but take it from me, it is no good getting settled in and then upsetting everyone as you scrimmage around looking for this and that.

Having reserved a bunk, I went outside — the evening was perfect, no wind and warm enough to enjoy a colourful Alpen-glow on the Monte Rosa Group of Mountains. When the sun had finally set we entered the hut and Ivo showed me where there were slippers to be worn instead of our heavy boots. The Guides have their own rooms for dining and sleeping so, after seeing that I was okay Ivo left me and I ordered a dinner that I thoroughly enjoyed. Apart from coffee and rye bread early next morning this will be your last nourishing meal until you return from your climb, so make the most of it.

All who intended climbing the next day retired to bed about 20.30 hours. I did not sleep well, thanks to a German snoring his head off, lucky devil, and my apprehension of the climb ahead. It was a long, long night brightened literally by a full moon that shone through the hut window. At about 03.30 hours the lights were switched on and I heard someone say it was a clear morning as I scrambled off my bunk. I dressed as quickly as possible but after I had put on my right boot I could feel what I thought was a *rucked* sock under my big toe. There was nothing for it but to unlace my boot and take off my socks and start again. This triviality possibly delayed me at least five minutes, and I ask myself what the outcome would have been had Ivo and I been five minutes higher at the time of our impending accident. By now Ivo had popped his head round the door to see how I was doing, naturally impatient having to wait. Eventually I got to the breakfast table, swallowed two cups of coffee, choked down some bread and jam, then roped up with Ivo who was not pleased at the delay in leaving the hut. Outside all was still, apart from the noise of climbers clambering up the path behind the hut. By now I was excited, my apprehension was behind me — this was it. At last I was on my way, within a few minutes I would actually be placing my feet on the rock face — actually doing what until now had just been a fantasy.

We both waited a few minutes to let other climbers clear the start, then it was our turn. From the start there was no mistaking what lay ahead. A sheer rock face up which shadowy figures were edging along ledges so narrow your boots overlapped the edge. There is a fixed wire rope to give you confidence and I was both thankful for this and at the same time flattered that Ivo was pressing on without stopping to belay me.

The Matterhorn is infamous for the loose rocks that abound everywhere, and it is for this reason that the Zermatt Guides prefer to lead the way to minimise the risk from falling stone etc., accidentally kicked down by climbers not used to the route.

Many experienced amateur climbers find it difficult, particularly in the dark, to follow the correct route on the Hornligrat. They are fortunate indeed if they can follow a guide with a beginner like myself, for should the guide have an experienced climber with him then it is likely that their pace will be too fast for the amateurs.

We must have been climbing for an hour or so when I glanced over my shoulder to see the dark jagged ridges of the Mischabel Group of Mountains with the night sky giving way to the rising sun. How I wished that we could

Fixed ropes on final ridge leading to summit snow slope. I had problems here!
Photo: Beat H. Perren.

The summit at last. Behind me is the Italian summit and metal cross.

Matterhorn Climber's badge.

have stopped so that I could photograph that wonderful sight. As it was, Ivo pressed on and I could only snatch a couple of pictures as we waited for other climbers to advance. I felt so full of confidence as the light improved — what a good thing we could not foretell the future!

Now we could see where we were going I noticed that we were ascending a steep gulley — what had been a steep scramble now turned into an interesting and exciting climb. The Guides were becoming impatient with a group of climbers making slow progress — I was not surprised, I had already made a mental note that the descent at this point was going to be a problem. Actually this section of the climb leads to the ridge from which you can look straight down on to the glacier at the base of the North face. In my opinion this part of the climb is the most interesting section below the Solvay Hut. The rest of the climb up to the Solvay Hut merged into a steady slog upwards. Several times we had to wait a few minutes for climbers to move on. At such times I took a few photographs but I could sense that Ivo had little time for photographers.

En route to the Solvay Hut we climbed the ÄLWE FAD an easy section leading to IM STEINSCHLAG where once again there was a danger from falling stones especially if climbers had taken the wrong route. Still higher there is a spot known as the ESELTRITTE where many years ago workmen bored holes into the rock when erecting a cable to carry materials to build the Solvay Hut.

Ivo next pointed out where the ALTE HUTTE was built before the Solvay Hut was erected. Not far from here there was a snow slope with a steep drop below. On the ascent, with the frozen snow, all was well but on my return 10 hours later it was a different story. We were fortunate as the steep ascent over the GIBISS leading to the UNTERE MOSELEY PLATTE was dry since this can become a difficult section if the rocks are icy.

On reaching the Solvay Hut we paused for a quick snack. Conditions were ideal — perfect blue sky showing off the FURGG RIDGE. I wish that on this occasion I had asked Ivo to show me the exposed North face just behind the hut, since a year later it was so cold I declined Ivo's offer to see this impressive view. Now we commenced the last half of the climb. It was approximately 07.45 —08.00 hours as we started up the perpendicular OBERE MOSELEY PLATTE named after an Americam climber Edward Oxnard Moseley who perished here in 1879. From here on it is interesting and energetic climbing — if you can keep going now without any acclimatization ill effects, you should make the summit. Shortly you mount the shoulder via the UNTERE ROTERTURM (Lower Red Tower). If there is any wind at all, particularly a North Westerly it will hit you here, however, on this climb (1979) conditions were good. Ivo now said that we should put on our crampons. In no time at all Ivo had his fixed and watched my fumbling efforts so it was he who deftly tightened my straps. If any real mountaineers are reading this I can just see their horror struck faces. Ivo asked me how I felt and I was able to re-assure him. I felt fine, thanks I am sure, to the way he had moderated his pace to my ability.

Eventually we crossed the SCHULTERGRAT (shoulder ridge) to the OBERER ROTERTURM — rocks leading to the start of the fixed ropes up the North face of the ridge. Climbers were now descending so the two way traffic made progress slow. The fixed ropes are in two distinct lengths FIXE SEILE IN DER NORDWAND — then up to the steepest part of the climb called AUF GRAD. Just below the Oberer Roterturm (Upper Red Tower) on the left can be seen a small cross known to the guides as ISIDORE CROSS, erected by guides in memory of a guide of that name who was killed in the 1930s.

Ivo and I had to wait on two narrow ledges halfway up the ridge on the North face. As we waited we heard a shout warning us of falling rocks, and I looked up and saw a blurred brown object hurtling out of a clear blue sky. It hissed by bringing with it a shower of smaller stones of which two hit my legs, but thanks to my snow gaiters I was not hurt. It was all over in seconds, and Ivo asked me if I was alright then said that he had been wounded on his head and arm. Ivo descended and sure enough his head was cut, nor seriously, but his right arm was a horrible mess. Fortunately he had no broken bones but the skin of his lower forearm had been folded back like a screwed up piece of paper. By this time we were joined by a guide and his client descending from the summit, so with the assistance of this guide Ivo bound his arm and stopped the bleeding. After a short discussion it was wisely decided that Ivo should not continue, and he suggested that he took over from the other guide and descend with his client whilst I was taken to the summit — 40 minutes away. It was ultimately decided that we should all descend with our own guide so here ended another attempt. However the story does not end here.

We returned to the Solvay Hut with Ivo keeping a tight rope on me despite his injured arm. At the Solvay Hut Ivo's arm was bandaged more thoroughly and we were invited to join two other *ropes* who united to assist *me* down the UNTERE MOSELEY PLATTE. I stress it was I who was grateful of this assistance since Ivo, despite his injured arm and head, was operating on all cylinders.

We continued our descent until we reached the snow slope mentioned earlier situated above the old hut. Before crossing this snow I pointed out to Ivo that the snow was now melting and I said that I thought the path would collapse as soon as I walked on it. Ivo replied that I must not lean inwards but outwards so off I went — then whoosh — there I was whizzing down the snow slope at a rate of knots on to the rocks below. Suddenly my fall was stopped with a jerk by the rope held firmly by Ivo, despite his wounded arm. I clambered back feeling very ashamed, so much for my ability to *lean out*.

The remainder of my descent was without incident except for the fact that the solo German climber, who kicked the rocks down, and spoiled my climb, followed Ivo and myself down the mountain (to think we, or rather Ivo was showing him the way!!) back to the hut where he was surrounded by hostile guides who failed to get any restitution.

This is yet another example why an inexperienced solo climber should employ a guide. A climber standing too near the summit edge is not just *inexperienced* he is a *menace*.

We were down by 13.30 hours so I took my time back to the Schwarzsee and Zermatt, and I eventually rounded the corner to our apartment about 16.00 hours to see Leita waiting anxiously on the balcony. My thumbs down sign upset her more than the chronicle of events had upset me. I realised how

This is to certify that

Mr. *Brian Bonner*

has climbed the Matterhorn

on the *1. September 1980*

The Guide Association of Zermatt

The President:

Kronig Emil

Kronig

The Guide:

Perren H.v.

The Certificate given after the ascent.

48

very, very fortunate Ivo and I were to return at all. As Ivo said later, *I do not think of what happened – only what might have happened.* Would those few minutes lost in adjusting my boot and sock have made any difference? Who knows?

It is very easy, particularly if you listen to well-meaning folk, to believe that setbacks such as I had experienced over the years were in fact Providence warning me. One's imagination so easily conjures up a fall, an injury, heart attack, or even death; the responsible, sensible part of you says *give it up – think of your family and be content with what you have achieved.*

Each day I had this battle within myself; however our daughter was now married and I kept telling myself that my wife would soon get over my absence (indeed she would be better off without me!) Oh yes, I had a great game of *kidology* and I won

ATTEMPT NO. 4 in July 1980, was doomed to failure as early as April and May of that year due to exceptionally cold weather experienced in England and the rest of Europe. At that time I can remember how difficult it was for the farmers to plough their land as the hard frost-bitten soil wore out their plough blades.

Remembering the marvellous weather enjoyed the previous July we booked our summer holidays for the same time i.e. first two weeks in July. As the Geneva — Brig express train sped up the Rhone valley I felt uneasy at the amount of snow on the surrounding mountain tops. Sure enough as we walked from Zermatt Railway Station I looked up at our mountain and realised immediately that there was far too much snow, for me at least, to think of climbing the Matterhorn. Actually the Belvedere Hut did not open until the last few days of our holiday, so I contented myself with a placid holiday photographing the superb alpine flowers. Yet another disappointment and financial setback. This obsession was becoming expensive.

ATTEMPT NO. 5, I suppose was a last desperate gamble — desperate but surely not the last? After the disappointing outcome of our July visit I brooded at home toying with the idea of snatching a week in Zermatt at the beginning of September. I had five precious days holiday that I could use, so I kept a wary eye on the television weather forecasts. On Tuesday, the 26th August I noticed that there was a high pressure area over Spain extending to Switzerland, with another high pressure area moving North East from the Bay of Biscay. I telephoned the London weather Centre who surprised me by saying it was wet in parts of Switzerland, including the Valais area, but this was expected to clear. Should I risk it?

My own physical condition was not as sound as I would have liked, having sprained a muscle in my left leg whilst jogging. Anyway, thanks to the co-operation of my staff agreeing to switch holidays, I decided to go. Wednesday, the 27th August was a busy day for Leita packing as I had been able to book a flight to Geneva from Heathrow Airport at 13.35 hours on Thursday, the 28th August. As it turned out it was a bad journey with our problems starting at Heathrow with an eighty minute flight delay which in turn made us miss our Geneva train. To top it all, as the Geneva airport bus lurched to a stop at the Railway Station it threw me sideways straining my suspect calf muscle. We eventually arrived in Zermatt at 22.36 hours and it was raining! The last straw was when an elastic strap on my luggage trolley sprang back and cut my nose. What a start! I will detail the rest of my story day by day.

Friday, 29th August 1980 — I must have woken about 06.00 hours and my first thought was whether my strained calf muscle in that left leg would trouble me. I looked out of the window at the Matterhorn and decided that the weather, though somewhat unsettled, could be worse. I had to become acclimatized as quickly as possible so I would have to push myself today and tomorrow. Leita said she would stay down in Zermatt and organise the home front, so I set off about 08.00 hours to climb the Oberrothorn via Ried, Tuftern and Tufternkumme as described earlier. I found the walk/scramble to the summit rather depressing as there was very little sunshine, in fact the Oberrothorn summit kept disappearing into the clouds and I was very pleased to join up with a German couple then descend with them to the Fluhalp. I was pleased my left leg stood up to the strain as I had been walking and climbing for 10 hours, taking in an ascent and descent of approximately 1,795m. I consoled myself thinking that the Matterhorn climb was 1,218m from the Belvedere Hut.

Saturday, 30th August 1980 — Today I had arranged to climb the Breithorn, so at 07.15 hours I was at the cable car station where I found that the guide allocated to take our party had abandoned the climb as it was raining. As you can imagine I was very annoyed when just an hour later the clouds broke, and for the whole day the Breithorn summit was in a clear blue sky. Anyway, I immediately decided to walk up to the Gornergrat — I just had to go as high as possible. The first part of the walk up to the Riffelalp was wet but very warm. Phew! how I perspired in my waterproofs and was I pleased that I had taken a small towel with which to dry myself. I maintained a fast pace cutting off many zig-zags and made a short diversion to visit the Riffelsee which is my favourite lake famous for its reflection of the Matterhorn but too often spoiled by wind and cloud. It was a little over 4 hours before I treated myself to a beer at the top. As I drank I mused over a visit there with Leita and Pat in 1971. What a thirst we all had on that occasion which we quenched with a whole bottle of Fendant wine with mineral water. Oh what a joke from there-on as the altitude and wine had its effect. How we raced back to Rotenboden without breaking our necks in a mystery! However, this time I continued to climb along the ridge called the Hohtalligrat leading up to the Stockhorn. If you are not a walker or climber you can make this memorable excursion on the Gornergrat Railway then take a cable car to the Stockhorn but take warm clothing.

As I had arranged to see Ivo that evening before dinner, I descended by train so ensuring I did not risk straining my knees on the descent, and also giving me plenty of time to discuss our plans with Ivo.

Ivo lives in a two storey chalet at the south end of the village looking straight up at the Matterhorn. What a superb position it is in. I would never get any work done I am sure if I lived there.

I cannot say that Ivo danced with delight when he saw me; no doubt he had memories of our last climb together, but nonetheless he had reserved the next three days for our Matterhorn climb.

Sunday, 31st August 1980 — I met Ivo as arranged at 11.00 hrs. outside the railway station and after a short discussion about the weather we decided to go up to the hut that afternoon. I returned to our apartment to pack and practice putting on my crampons. I gave my leg a last dip in hot and cold water as I seemed to remember that this treatment was good for sprains.

At last I was ready and impatient to go. Leita walked with me to the cable car station and waved us off. Not so many were travelling at this time of day since most were descending, it being 15.00 hrs.

As we left the shelter of the Schwarzsee cable car station, it was **very** cold with a strong icy wind blowing from the north west. We made good time and arrived at the hut in 1 hour 35 minutes which pleased Ivo (about the last time I did please him!).

Compared with our attempt last year, the weather was bitterly cold. No sitting outside the hut to enjoy the last rays of sun this time — each time the door to the Belvedere Hut opened a stream of hot air *steamed* out. I ventured from the warmth of the hut for a few minutes to photograph an apology for an Alpen-glow and wondered whether such an evening was a harbinger of bad weather tomorrow. I hoped not. I soon returned to the warmth of the stove at the back of the hut and changed into a pair of slippers which I had grabbed from the rack near the front door.

As I ate my supper I made friends with a young German couple from Essen who were staying the night in order to enjoy the atmosphere of the hut. Although they did not intend to climb the Matterhorn they must have been up early the next morning as they sent me a telephoto photograph of our party and others climbing up to the Solvay Hut as the sun was rising. I also met an American who was extraordinarily lucky. He had sold his business in America and was on an extended European holiday. He had just arrived in Zermatt from Norway and Germany and had gone straight up to the Belvedere Hut expecting to find a guide for the Matterhorn. Normally one has to reserve a guide at the Guides' Office in Zermatt, but on this particular evening a guide had come all the way from St. Luke to meet a client only to find that through a misunderstanding a Zermatt guide had also been engaged. The American was therefore able to climb the next morning, and although we did not exchange names, we did exchange occupations. Lucky man, he achieved within 24 hours of seeing the Matterhorn what was taking me 15 years!

I turned in at 8.30 p.m. (20.30 hrs.) to find that I was the last, and again I had a top bunk sleeping no better on this occasion than I did on the last. As it was so cold I wore my woollen winter vest, woollen pullover and climbing socks and tried, without much success, to wrap the two blankets round me. At last I was settled and I must have dozed off for an hour or two and then of course the *call of nature* beckoned. Fortunately my torch was to hand so down I struggled and groped my way along a freezing corridor to a damp wooden seat covering a hole that went straight down to the glacier beneath. Hanging over the throne was a notice that proudly proclaimed *Pissoir*. Eventually I crawled back to my bunk, and how the other occupants must have cursed me as first one, then another and yet another made their way to that exalted toilet!

Monday, 1st September 1980 — AT 04.00 hrs. I was off that bunk in a shot and dressed as quickly as I could — to hell with any rucks in my socks! Downstairs, breakfast was laid out on the tables — a bottle of Nescafé, hot water, small cartons of milk and jam. We helped ourselves and I was the first to leave the table. Ivo was ready to rope me up and within 5 minutes we were the first guided party away. No messing this time folks!

The cold wind was still with us and I regretted not putting on my extra pullover from the start, but otherwise it was a perfect morning. The steep rock climb at the beginning was a known factor this time so we made fast progress without belaying.

I was wearing open-ended woollen gloves because the year before I needed to feel with my fingers for the handholds. I should have worn thick waterproof woollen mittens as I found that my finger ends, protruding out of my woollen gloves, were freezing to the rock face, and in as matter of seconds I had to pluck my fingers off the rock. It must have been at this early stage of the climb that four fingers on my left hand suffered from first degree frostbite.

Despite the cold I ws enjoying the climb. Perhaps I am asking to be contradicted here but I would say that 85% of the climb is very steep, but not technically difficult PROVIDED the rocks are free from ice. The remaining 15% is literally straight up!

Although Ivo and I overtook several amateur climbers we were now being overtaken by guides climbing quicker than ourselves. It slowly became lighter and the sight of the sun below the mountains to the east was a wonderful as ever. As I gazed I noticed two climbers silhouetted against the sunrise. It was a classical picture often seen on Alpine calendars so I reached for my camera, but no sooner did Ivo see my intention than he told me, in no uncertain manner, that I either climbed the Matterhorn OR take photographs. If the latter, then he would take me down, so suitably chastened I continued the climb. As I looked up, the very top of the summit was a delicate pink —and I will now divulge — I sneaked a photograph.

Despite the sun rise, it was as cold as ever but roped up as I was and constantly on the move there never seemed to be an opportune moment to put on my pullover which was still in the rucksack. No doubt it was the bitter cold, but I felt that the climb was harder this year and I was pleased to see the Solvay Hut perched on its ledge some 500 feet above. I was surprised that this time Ivo did not stop for a breather or refreshment but pressed on for the second half of the climb.

Some three hundred feet above the Solvay hut we paused to fix our crampons. Now, I thought, I will show just how good I am after all the time spent practising this exercise. Well, I did show him, but what a pathetic attempt it was with Ivo having to restrap each foot, and even then one crampon fell off on the descent. Just here I thought *now this is where a lot of climbers suffer ill effects from acclimatization*, fortunately I felt fine but my movements were not as quick as the year before.

Shortly after we recommenced climbing, the rope attaching me to Ivo brushed my spectacles and knocked off my clip-on sunglasses.

I called out and we stopped for me to retrieve them but unfortunately they just slipped out of reach, and the bitter north west wind blew them down a couloir. Mentally I waved them goodbye, or so I thought! I was wearing my Balaclava helmet as a hat and a few minutes later this too blew off and disappeared down the east face — it was a bad 5 minutes. Let the lessons be learned:- Put on your Balaclava helmet properly. Do not use clip-on sun glasses. If your sight will allow, wear snow goggles or, as I did on the Rimpfischhorn, wear spectacles with tinted lenses that adjust to light intensity. You can obtain plastic side shields that are fitted securely to your spectacle frame. Climbing in the cold wearing spectacles does create problems particularly of misting but I would think that one could treat the lenses in some way to overcome this.

We were now well up on the shoulder and the bitterly cold wind was creating spindrift conditions with the fine particles of snow blowing into my eyes like small needles. Here Ivo lent me a spare Balaclava helmet which he was carrying and I was most grateful I can tell you.

Now we came to the first fixed rope on the edge of the north face which made me realise that my pre-climb training had omitted an important factor — I had neglected to strengthen my arms, which I could have done with a few press ups each night as well as the knees bend routine. I think most climbers will have no difficulty with handling the ropes as my weakness was caused, as previously mentioned, through a broken elbow suffered many years ago. The recent snow fall had been blown clear by the force of the wind exposing rock that had to support the crampons. If I had been more experienced I would have tried to climb in a sideways manner, as it was, I used the two front spikes on the crampon and this put a heavy strain on my legs. Yes, you have guessed it, that suspect calf muscle gave me hell. As we passed the spot where we turned back last time Ivo motioned with his hands. I wonder what his thoughts were? Possibly he did not give it a second thought, I just prayed that this time we would have better luck.

At this stage of the ascent we were climbing the final steep ridge and I estimate that we were some 45 minutes from the summit, and my nose seemed to be glued to the rock face as the fixed ropes took us over a number of very steep pitches. Ivo was, of course, ahead but out of sight. The rock face seemed perpendicular and my frozen hands and weak arms slipped on the rope as my body approached the ridge I had to get over. Ivo shouted *what is the matter?* Again I hauled myself to the tip of the ledge, only to slide back, but this time I saw Ivo and heard him shout and gesticulate that I should use the chain that I now saw — a fixed looped chain on the left just below the ledge. One more try, and this time, instead of sliding back, I looped my left arm through the chain and with one more scrambled heave I was over. It seems that at this particular spot, where the chain is now fixed, there was once a good handhold but this had been removed with the mistaken motive that if the route was made more difficult there would be a greater demand for guides. Actually it prevented guides from climbing in band weather so the chain was fixed to redress the situation.

Purists can argue with conviction that articifical aids abuse the sport of mountaineering, but I for one am grateful for all the assistance I can get. Heaven forbid though that there should ever be a lift or cable car to the summit.

Ahead was the final snow slope, steep enough to cause me to use my hands as well as my feet. Climbing on all fours, I must have caused a smile. My eyes were still smarting and all I could see was a blur of snow, when suddenly by my side I heard the voice of my Amercan furniture-maker saying *keep going Banker, you are only five minutes from the summit.* I needed no second bidding and within five minutes we were there. (Now you know my occupation!).

As far as I can remember, Ivo asked what I thought and I replied that all we had to do now was to get down. I am sure he must have been disappointed at my reaction but the view of the distant peaks were spoilt as my eyes would not focus clearly on objects. I was paying the price for losing my sun glasses.

This was a great shame and made photography most difficult, but Ivo took the all-important photograph of myself on the summit — this incidentally was slightly scratched in processing — Mamma mia! I clicked off several more photographs and turned my attention to the summit ridge some two yards wide, dropping sheer towards Italy, with a very steep slope down to the north and east faces. I remember thinking, this must be the slope where the accident occurred with Edward Whymper 115 years ago. I was sorry that we did not get closer to the Italian summit with its splendid cross but conditions did not encourage us to linger and it was with some trepidation that I gripped the fixed rope to climb down the rock face that had given me so many problems earlier. Ivo's advice was to *stand off* the rope. I did my best but it was a clumsy descent and I was grateful for the tight belay Ivo maintained. I have always preferred the ascent to the descent and this was no exception. On the shoulder once more the wind seemed even colder, no doubt a certain amount of tiredness was setting in. Suddenly a crampon came loose, my numb fingers were unable to fasten it to Ivo's satisfaction. Lower down it was with relief that I took off my crampons and relied on my vibram soles, but very soon I had lost confidence in those because I seemed to slip flat on my back as soon as any wet rock sloped too steeply. Because I was constantly slipping, my back became bruised so it was difficult to bend forward which did not help matters.

Now we were descending the Obere Moseley Platte and it was necessary to turn in and face the rock. Here you must secure yourself with hand and footholds but finding the latter is not easy. Although this pitch cannot be considered difficult a certain dexterity and ability to stretch is a decided advantage.

We rested for ten minutes in the Solvay Hut and Ivo unroped and went outside, returning a few minutes later holding out my sun glasses. This just showed how intimately he knew his mountain. He offered me a drink of tea and red wine, considered by Ivo to be the most sustaining drink to take.

The rest of the descent to the base of the mountain was slow and tiring, and although I was full of admiration for the way Ivo had brought me down, his constant urgings to go faster did get on my nerves. I was tired and the obstacles to be overcome seemed never-ending, I found the last hour of the climb to be the most nerve-racking. At last you can see there is only 50 feet to go and this time I was belayed as I edged along the final four inch ledge, holding on to the fixed rope. Just before jumping down on to *terra firma* I heard Ivo shout something, I did not hear what it was but I landed on an icy surface, nearly falling flat on my back, so he must have been warning me of ice. It was 16.15 hrs. and we were down. Ivo shook my hand and I thanked him for bringing me back in one piece, at the same time apologising for my clumsiness.

We had to bend almost double to fight the buffeting wind as we struggled to the Belvedere Hut entrance. The Matterhorn was not patting me on the back and saying *well done* — it was throwing me back with a strong reminder that this was a mountain able to conjure up its own gales and storms.

As we entered the hut, the heat and stuffiness hit us, my spectacles misted up and I could not see a thing in the gloom. It was now 16.55 hrs. and the last cable car from the Schwarzsee was timed, so I thought, at 17.25 hrs. Ivo said that he would hurry off to catch the last cable car, meanwhile I telephoned Leita to tell her my good news, and to warn her that I would have to spend another night at the Belvedere Hut.

Now it was all over I was in an emotional state as I spoke to Leita, but I soon pulled myself together and made my way back to the common room where I was amazed to see Ivo. *Why are you still here?* I asked, and Ivo replied that a load of logs was to be delivered to the hut within a few minutes by helicopter and he was to fly back to Zermatt with them. Needless to say I asked if there would be room for me so Ivo said that he would ask the pilot. The helicopter made 4 trips with a huge load of logs hanging beneath in a rope sling. To watch Ivo stacking those logs you would not have thought he had been 12 hours on the Matterhorn with a *beginner*.

After the 4th trip the helicopter landed on a rock behind the hut and as the pilot came down Ivo asked him if I could return with them to Zermatt. I was lucky as the pilot agreed and said that we should get into the helicopter immediately. As we waited, the craft was rocked by the gale that was increasing in force. Later Ivo told me that the pilot had doubts about taking off — good thing I was not aware of this! Eventually the pilot returned with his sheaf of papers, climbed into his seat, slammed the door shut and started the turbo engine. The whine of the engine increased and the rotor arm spun at what seemed to be a very slow speed so I was not expecting the take off when it happened. Suddenly the whole glacier went topsy-turvy and we banked away from the hut and shot off towards Zermatt. Within five minutes we had landed at the Heliport and I arranged to meet Ivo the next morning.

Our apartment is a 10 minute walk from the Heliport so within 30 minutes of 'phoning Leita from the Belvedere Hut I was ringing the door bell. Surprise, surprise, *Good Lord how did you get here, have you flown?*

Leita soon had me relaxing in a hot bath with a cup of tea resting on the toilet seat alongside — that bath was sheer bliss. We enjoyed a celebration dinner and I decided to make it an early night.

I was still having trouble with my eye sight so as Ivo had recommended placing used tea bags over the eye lids, I took his advice and looked a *proper Charley* with tea trickling down my cheeks. I did not sleep until about 3 a.m. when Leita brought me a cup of hot chocolate which was just what I needed to get me off to sleep. Right to the end Leita was there — she was wonderful. The next morning I felt fine. The only visible signs of my climb were 4 black tips on my left hand showing just how cold it had been up there, and a bruised back.

At the Guides' Office I received congratulations from Emil Kronig who solemnly scribed a diploma signed by himself and Ivo stating that Brian

Bonner climbed the Matterhorn on the 1st September, 1980. He also presented me, for a small fee, with the Matterhorn Climbers' Badge.

After the presentation Ivo and I adjourned for a coffee and I settled my debts, or did I? Naturally one pays the listed tariff for the climb plus the cost of staying in the Hut, but when you know that it is only due to the skill of your guide that you can tell the tale — what is that worth? Whatever is given in thanks will be insufficient; how does one put a monetary value on one's life?

When it was truly over my feelings were mixed. After 33 years of dreaming and 15 years of striving it had been achieved. All along I had realised that it could only be done with the help of a guide willing to nurse me along, and Ivo did just that. If only I had been fitter, if only I could have completed the climb in 1979 when I was fitter and the weather was warmer. If only I had been able to climb in July, 1980, when I had no suspect leg muscle and I had trained longer in Zermatt instead of just 3 days. There were all those IFS with just one BUT:-

I GOT THERE.

CHAPTER 7

THE EASY WAY

Back home I carefully packed and posted my precious photographs to a well known international company for processing. I must mention, since I will never forgive or forget this company, that after our abortive holiday in July 1979, I posted my transparencies to the same company and had them returned badly scratched. You would have thought, after such an experience, that I would have used a different make of film, but I mistakenly thought that lightning did not strike twice in one spot. However I did make a point of telephoning the company asking for extra careful treatment. Believe it or not my slides were returned for the second time badly damaged. As I actually received a letter acknowledging the negligence of an employee I should have sued but was not prepared to risk having to pay legal costs. The result of all this was I did not have sufficient transparencies to make a colour slide presentation. At the same time I was aware that an audience would be unable to appreciate the size and conditions on the mountain as my range of photographs was limited. Remember Ivo had realised that all my time and energy would be required to climb without messing about with camera-lenses etc.

After a short discussion with Leita it was decided there was one excellent way to rectify my shortage of pictures, and this was by hiring a helicopter to fly us up the route I had climbed.

We arrived once more in Zermatt on Saturday, 4th July 1981, after a tense flight when our BA Tristar turned back to Heathrow only 15 minutes from Geneva with its port engine closed down through loss of oil pressure. We were given flight priority at Heathrow and as we descended Leita nudged my arm and pointed out of the window. I took a deep breath and gripped her hand tighter because there on the runway every few hundred yards stood ambulances and fire engines. We eventually took off again in a different Tristar and, much to our relief, arrived in Geneva some 4 hours late.

The weather, always the most important factor in Zermatt, was unsettled. The mornings started with a very low cloud base but cleared by mid-day consequently I did not book a Helicopter flight with Air Zermatt thinking that the Matterhorn would be in the clouds. I could not have been more wrong. The mountain was climbed each day as the summit was way above the cloud ceiling. On hearing this news I went to the Guides' Office and renewed my acquaintance with Emil Kronig. It was very important from a photographic point of view that there should be climbers on the summit when our helicopter was hovering above. This would be a gamble since conditions could make the climbers later than they intended.

Conditions seemed right for Tuesday 14th July, and Emil said he thought climbers should be near or on the summit by 09.15 hrs. so I booked a flight for 09.00 hrs. As there was room for four passengers we invited Ivo to accompany us, and to reduce costs I sold the fourth seat to a Swiss from Zurich.

Tuesday dawned fine with the usual plumage of clouds on the Matterhorn summit and a fair amount of wispish cloud over the Visptal Valley. I kitted myself up with three cameras:- A Rollei 35T, my old faithful Fuji ST701 with 50 mm. lens, and I borrowed a Fuji 605 with a 200 mm. Pentax lens. The latter proved quite useless owing to the speed of the helicopter making it impossible to focus, so I changed back to the 50 mm. lens.

We arrived in good time at the heliport situated a short distance outside Zermatt to the north, and did not have to wait long for the helicopter to sweep in from the Theodule glacier where two skiers had been dropped. As we hurried forward to climb into our seats I took a photograph which caused a problem later as I will explain.

I took the seat next to the pilot and immediately we were off, banking sharply round to fly down the Visptal valley to Täsch, gaining height as we flew.

Over Täsch I saw the large car park filled with what seemed to be *Dinky* toy cars, then suddenly we climbed into cloud and occasionally glimpsed the side of the Mettelhorn which seemed much too near for comfort and I hoped all would be well. Within seconds we were over the ridge making for the Weisshorn glacier — then we swung south and the thrill of the flight was so great we all gasped with wonder at the views we obtained as we slid over ravines, ridges, and glaciers towards the Hornli and Belvedere huts.

Within five minutes we were hovering over the Hornli and Belvedere Huts then flew quickly up to the Solvay hut where we could see climbers starting the steep rock face immediately above the hut. The pilot hovered long enough for me to take photographs, then swept over the Hornli ridge to the north face. As I looked back I hurriedly snapped a picture of the Solvay hut perched in its rocky cleft. I don't suppose any of us will have such an experience again — the thrill of the flight was tremendous, although I think it was appreciated more by my companions than myself, since I was concentrating on the views through the camera lens so missed the awesome majesty of the whole scene. As the rotor blades overhead maintained their comforting rhythm we gained height and floated back over the shoulder where the pilot closed in to enable me to photograph climbers on the fixed ropes ascending the very steep rock face before the final snow slope to the summit. Finally we rose to look down on to climbers still struggling up to the summit and on the summit.

We now flew slowly along the summit ridge and noticed just before the cross on the Italian summit, tracks in the snow made by climbers who had conquered the north face — now that is something to be proud of — but not for the likes of me. Before leaving the summit we flew over the Zmuttgrat Ridge which made me very much aware why the Hornligrat route is so popular. How I wish that I had started climbing forty years ago. As we looked back at the short snow hump that is the Matterhorn summit we saw a lone figure through the hazy clouds. As much as I admired this lone figure's achievement I thought at the same time, *Yes, it was the likes of you who damn nearly killed Ivo and myself in 1979.*

When we banked away from the summit I expected our pilot to return to the Heliport, but he certainly gave us value for money as he decided to demonstrate the versatility of his helicopter over the glacier at the base of the 4,091 m. mountain called Pollux which I have since climbed with Ivo. Pillars of ice and snow rushed towards us, then over we would pop, turning at the same time, causing the whole glacier seemingly to climb on top of us. Many more times we zoomed over crevasses; at times the rotor blades, instead of revolving overhead, were revolving in front of our eyes — it was terrific — then a short period of normal flight back to the landing pad.

As we climbed out we were chattering like a group of excited children who had been taken on a great adventure. I have heard the expression of being *high* and believe me, we must all have been in that state and it took a good 30 minutes and a coffee to quieten us down.

Now in our apartment I began to unload my cameras, and to my great consternation I noticed that one of the cameras that had been *pre-set* (exposure meters give false readings at high altitude and in snow) was set incorrectly. Remember the photograph I took as we entered the helicopter? Well, in my excitement I did not re-adjust the exposure setting. *Leita* I stammered *I will have to go again.*

I will not repeat Leita's reply, but buying off her wrath with the promise of a Swiss cardigan I arranged a re-run the next day. However, on this second flight, I could only take pot luck with the seating arrangements as I could not afford to charter the helicopter on my own as before.

Anyway, I was very fortunate as I managed once more to sit next to the pilot and obtain uninterrupted views, but this time I was handed a headset which enabled the pilot to give me a commentary and answer questions on the flight.

The second flight differed from the first and turned out to be much more circumspect. We did not spend so much time on the Hornligrat route but as the wind had dropped we did fly right round the Matterhorn, across to the Kleine Matterhorn, over the Breithorn, Pollux, skirted the Monte Rosa making for the Adler Pass. I will always remember the depth of the snow here, layer after layer. I was particularly pleased with the quality of my pictures, always a gamble for me, especially one showing the Rimpfischhorn since I climbed this with Ivo in 1983 and can thoroughly recommend this climb for novices with a good guide.

Sorry, I have diverged somewhat from the flight. Oh yes, way way down in the valley of Saas I could see the winding road leading to Saas Grund and Saas Fee before we swung back to Zermatt past the Michabeljock SAC hut and Täschhorn.

This time as I climbed from the helicopter a German speaking Swiss came up to me and put 10 francs into my hand saying *drinken, drinken* and gesturing in the appropriate manner. Naturally I attempted to return the money but he insisted. Later as we drank a coffee and Schnapps I exchanged my address with my donor. Much, much, later that day, as I was telling Leita of the Swiss gentleman's kind action, I was smitten with the reason for his generosity. As I was wearing headphones and talking to the pilot he thought I was aircrew! I did feel an imposter, and when I sent him photographs of the flight made it clear who I really was.

CHAPTER 8

THE AFTERMATH
1982
POLLUX

At the beginning I expressed an opinion that climbing in the Alps should not be allied simply to a passing fancy that prompts you to borrow a pair of boots to climb the Matterhorn and then retire to the Golf Course. I think I can say, now I have fulfilled my obsession, that my burning desire to climb the Matterhorn has changed to a sincere wish to maintain some semblance of physical fitness to climb mountains of any size.

I enjoy planning climbs I often never start! When I meet Ivo in Zermatt I am brought down to reality. So it happened in 1982 when we decided to climb POLLUX 4091 m. (13,422 ft.) This choice was influenced by the fact that thanks to the Luftseilbahn up to the Kleine Matterhorn this climb can be done without staying overnight at a mountain hut. However I must say a climb does not seem complete without the experience of staying at a hut.

I can remember meeting Ivo at 07.00 hours outside the Luftseilbahn station in Zermatt. We joined 2 or 3 other guides with their clients, most of whom were climbing the Breithorn, all were undecided whether to go as the weather seemed unsettled. As it was the last day of the summer time table it was, so far as I was concerned, today or not at all that year, consequently Ivo decided to go and the other guides then seemed to make the same decision. Actually the threatening clouds lifted and at the Kleine Matterhorn we were in brilliant sunshine.

The journey up in the cable car always excites me. Most of my fellow passengers were skiers all colourfully dressed in expensive boots and clothing — a contrast to my battered boots and climbing gear. At Furi and Furgg we clomped from one car to another, and I snatched an impressive photograph at Furgg of the east face of the Matterhorn. (Try to do this if you can since on the descent you will be tired and the sun will have moved westwards). After our tickets had been examined by the ticket collector and he had confirmed on the intercom that all was ready we were swung upwards on the final stage of the journey. As we approached the Kleine Matterhorn we looked down on to the serrated surface of the Theodule Glacier and its impressive seracs. Slowly the car eased into the concrete bay and we were disgorged into the freezing tunnel that leads from the centre of the Kleine Matterhorn to the Breithorn Plateau. Without a doubt the construction of this cable car system from Trockener Steg 2929 m. to Kleine Matterhorn 3820 m. is one of the world's finest engineering feats. At this altitude pressure cookers will not function and it takes an age to boil water — only come to this height if you are sound in lung and heart. During the construction it was found that due to the low oxygen content of the atmosphere, output of work per man was only 50 to 75 per cent of that at normal level.

What a contrast it was to walk from the gloom of the tunnel into a dazzling snowy fairy land. Immediately to our left of the exit was a void filled with white fluffy clouds stretching away to the north and west with just the highest mountain peaks jutting through the clouds. Ivo, as always, tied me expertly to his neatly coiled rope, put on his gloves and haversack then set off with me at a respectful distance at the rear. Our way followed the ski route for a short time before bearing away from the Breithorn route and towards the Breithorn Pass. Ahead, a little to our right, was the domed head of Castor with the summit of Pollux somewhat nearer to our left. Care was needed as we crossed numerous small crevasses and I was able to photograph 3 climbers ahead gingerly prodding their way carefully over, what appeared to me to be fragile snow bridges linking the two sides of each crevasse. Eventually we overtook the three climbers and, although I did not know it at the time, this was the start of a good friendship with Hermann Bär and his wife Helen. It took about 1½ hours to reach the loose rocky morraine at the base of Pollux, and it was here we had a short rest and I tried to change my film. *Tried* is the operative word as I lost the end of the film by accidentally winding it into the cassette. I was, to put it mildly, very annoyed since that finished my photographic ambitions. We were making for the small snow plateau leading to the final snow ridge, sliding and scrambling across steep slopes. Within another 20 minutes we were on the summit with an exciting panorama of Glaciers and Peaks all round us. *My Kingdom for a camera* I thought however I was lucky because on our way down we met Hermann and Helen Bär with their guide. I asked Hermann if he would take a picture of Ivo and me with the summit of Pollux in the background. I had the temerity to ask if an allowance had been made to the exposure to compensate for reflected light from the snow. I remember Helen stating with some emphasis that I had nothing to worry about *as my Husband takes good pictures*. Much later, after exchanging addresses and photographs, I discovered that Hermann was the Proprietor of FOTO BAREN OPTIK a well known camera shop in Zurich. In addition his Cannon cameras were serviced annually by Cannon in recognition of his superb colour slide presentations!

After leaving Mr, and Mrs. Bär, Ivo asked me to descend a sheer rock face on which there was a small diagonal crack with a wire to hold on to. Although there was only fifty or sixty feet of descent I can remember I was thankful Ivo had a tight rope on me. On this occasion, as many times in the past, I kept my fingers crossed until Ivo was alongside. By now the sun was at its highest and Ivo must have thought the snow ridges over the crevasses could have weakened, so he attached a loop of rope to my body rope explaining that if I fell into a crevasse I should put a foot into the loop so I could be pulled out with greater ease. Fortunately there was no mishap but it was warm work trudging up the soft snow to the Breithorn Pass. We made good time and caught a cable car down to Zermatt earlier than expected. As we drank our lager in Zermatt Mr. and Mrs. Bär arrived and I was immediately impressed by their wonderful sense of humour.

1983
THE RIMPFISCHHORN

The most satisfying climb with Ivo, since our 1980 Matterhorn success, was in 1983 when we climbed the Rimpfischhorn 4,199 m. (13,776 ft.). This ascent from the Fluhalp mountain hut 2,616 m. entails a total climb of 1583 m. (5,194 ft.) which, rather surprisingly, is some 365 m. (1,198 ft.) more than the height between the Belvedere Hut and Matterhorn summit.

We set off for the Fluhalp mountain hut at 16.30 hrs. on 5th SEPTEMBER. It was a warm sunny afternoon and I could not help comparing my relaxed attitude to the climb with my feelings almost exactly 3 years before when Ivo and I left Zermatt for the Matterhorn. We used the new railway, burrowed out of solid rock, that rushes you through the bowels of the earth up to the Sunnegga station. Apart from the fact that before you board the train you pass through a special air lock, you could be catching a London tube train! Quite horrible. Such a contrast to the now disused Sunnegga Sesselbahn that used to whisk you quietly over the tree tops with wonderful glimpses of marmots, alpine flowers and mountains — so much for progress. To avoid arriving at the Fluhalp in a hot sticky state Ivo favoured the use of the Luftsellbahn that swung us up in small cabins to the Blauherd Station where we disembarked. From the station it is a pleasant stroll past a small lake called the Stellisee. This spot is very popular with photographers as the lake is surrounded by a huge rock garden of alpine flowers, and if there is no wind to ripple the water a fine reflection of the Matterhorn can be obtained. Away to the north east the twin peaks of the Rimpfischhorn could be seen against a cloudless blue sky. Oh I did pray that the weather would hold — alas I could not have prayed with sufficient conviction.

On arrival at the Fluhalp hut we took off our boots and relaxed in slippers that were provided, as our evening meal was being prepared. There was another group of climbers who asked Ivo if he would take a rope with one up the Matterhorn but allow a second rope of three to follow him. Ivo refused explaining that at that time of year there would not be sufficient time to wait for the rope of three to keep up with him. I fully appreciated why the suggestion was not feasible since it had taken Ivo and me 12 hours to complete the climb. We retired to bed about 20.45 hrs. and as there was no other guide in the hut with clients, Ivo shared the same dormitory as myself although normally the guides tend to keep to themselves. What a night! We left the window on the latch despite a strong wind that suddenly blew up after a sunset that gave doubts about the weather next day. Each time I moved, the bunk creaked so before long I climbed out and tried to secure it. Then every gust made the door rattle so I climbed out again to stuff a handkerchief in the door. Eventually I sparodically dozed. Each time I woke, I looked out of the window vainly looking for stars to indicate that the sky was clear. At last my wrist watch alarm sounded but although it was only 3 o'clock I still got up, took my torch as all lighting had been switched off until the Warden was up, crept down to the bathroom then proceeded to lose my torch in the toilet, it had rolled under the partition. Great start! By the time I returned and dressed, Ivo was ready. I should add that we were still in the dark as this fact nearly had disastrous consequences later! Shortly the lights were switched on and we snatched a quick breakfast of Nescafe, Rye Bread and butter before roping up and stepping into the darkness.

I was thankful that Ivo knew the way and I had a good torch. Within 20 minutes we began to clamber upwards over what turned out to be the debris from a huge avalanche. Shortly we overtook the climbers we had met at the hut the night before, and I know they were thankful to be able to follow Ivo and myself as it was still very dark and impossible to see the faint track. We eventually reached the beginning of the glacier and put on our crampons. Ivo dislikes wearing crampons and discards them at the first opportunity, but I am much happier with them on, since I am incapable of walking downhill on ice. I have to admit I am a pitiful sight and Ivo cannot understand my problem. (I wish I did.)

This huge glacier the *Langfluegletscher* seemed to bug me all day. It twisted and turned with one rocky outcrop after another; it seemed never ending. The weather was disappointing as one of the highlights of this climb should have been the sunrise ahead of us. As it was we just kept our heads down into a biting wind with the cloud base getting nearer and nearer. Fortunately I was snug and warm as Ivo had kindly lent me a pair of long cotton pants that kept me warm but not too warm on the descent when the sun broke through. Now comes the big BUT!! as we paused to relieve ourselves I could not find the essential part of my anatomy. Where was it? After feverish groping I realized that in the dark as I dressed I had put the pants on back to front. Oh well you live and learn.

Shortly after the pants' crisis the weather began to improve and as the cloud base lifted, so did my spirits. The next obstacle was a bastion of rock leading to the upper glacier, as I glanced back I saw two other ropes of climbers moving over the lower glacier and it was noticeable that one group was slower than the other. Once on the upper glacier the clouds began to break up and I was pleased to see, through gaps in the ever shifting clouds, the summits of Monte Rosa and Liskamm. We paused to admire the constantly changing views, when suddenly three climbers appeared, over the edge of the rocks we had climbed, underneath a small rainbow caused by the sun rays falling on a local snow shower — just a flash of beauty, here one moment and then nothing. The climbers were obviously fit and going well, and soon they were out of sight over a snow ridge which indicated that for a time at least we would be descending. Sure enough, as we breasted the ridge we saw the tracks dropping down several hundreds of feet to the steep snow slope leading up to the final rock climb. When we finally reached the slope we had to zig zag our way upwards taking care not to overbalance. We were approximately at 13,200 ft. (say 4000 m.) and Ivo asked how I felt. Whenever I receive any solicitude from Ivo I know I can expect trouble or distress. Sure enough I had to signal him to wait as I inhaled deeply before battling on a dozen more steps. At such times I feel so grateful to be allowed to enjoy (?) such physical efforts. Fortunately, apart from shortage of breath due to the altitude, I felt well. At last we reached solid rock covered in a thick hoar frost. That day the last rope of climbers we had seen making slow progress on the lower glacier gave up at this point due to the icy conditions, and without Ivo I would certainly have done the same. As it was we continued confidently upwards moving one at a time. Unfortunately clouds obliterated the exposed S.E. ridge overlooking the Adler Pass and the Adlerhorn, this may have been a blessing as I could not see the sheer drop beneath us.

I was climbing comfortably then suddenly we were on the secondary summit looking down a steep but easy ridge to a small col (depression-saddle-pass) between ourselves and the final summit. As we looked we saw the three climbers almost on the summit. Within fifteen minutes we had joined their company, the time was 10.30 a.m. It was a good thing we were not more than five on the summit since a convenient V shaped cleft provided just sufficient room and protection to enable all to appreciate the superb views to the north and west, however the view to the south was obliterated by persistent cloud. Whenever I am on an Alpine summit there seems to be a cold wind and the Rimpfischhorn summit was no exception, so Ivo moved along the cleft to a sheltered ledge situated just over the edge where he suggested we had lunch. Before unpacking our haversacks, Ivo was careful to belay us both as boiling grey clouds continued to swirl beneath us and conceal our exposed position. Before descending I took several photographs, the most impressive showing the minor summit ridge with a climber silhouetted against the sky line. Ivo pointed out the neighbouring Allalinhorn and the Italian St. Margareta hut on Monte Rosa.

On the descent Ivo kept an extremely tight rope on me as we gingerly climbed down the rocks still covered with ice and frost. I am pleased to say that on this climb I had no slips **on rock**, however there was one problem that nearly spoiled my day. Ivo had arranged for his wife Hermine and Leita to meet us at the Fluhalp hut at 14.30 hrs. Now if Ivo says he will be back at a certain time then nothing will stand in his way — certainly not a slithering Bonner unable to stand on his two feet. If I had retained my crampons there would have been no problem, as it was I kept falling down until I just had to ask Ivo to slow down which he did — just a little! Eventually we got off the glacier about 13.45 hrs. Down, down, we clambered at a good pace over the remains of the ancient avalanche, and I was amazed how Ivo had been able to lead everyone up so quickly earlier that morning. Ivo seemed pleased enough to arrive back at the hut just four minutes late. My word! it was a relief to sit down and drink a bowl of soup I can remember, as if it was yesterday, how good that soup tasted.

Later in 1983 Ivo and Hermine were our guests for 5 days in Hornsea N. Humberside and we were able to show them the impressive coastal and moorland scenery of North Yorkshire.

1984 was a disappointing year. We moved from Hornsea to Oxfordshire hoping to live in softer climes and nearer to our family, but the high cost of property in that area thwarted our plans which meant we were unable to visit Zermatt that year.

Lower peak of Rimpfischhorn from summit.

Approaching the Theodule Pass and Italian Alpine hut on Italian-Swiss border. The Furgggrat (Furgg ridge) (average height 3350m. 10,944ft.) links the Matterhorn to the Pass.

1985
ZERMATT — TÄSCH HUT — TÄSCH

In 1985 Leita threw down the gauntlet and stated "I've had enough of Zermatt. I don't mind you going to Zermatt to climb with Ivo but I don't enjoy hanging around the shops whilst you are away climbing." This is how I came to be in Zermatt in September without Leita. Fortunately Hermann and Helen Bär were on holiday in Zermatt at the same time, so I enjoyed their companionship during the evenings, and on a memorable trip together to the *Täsche Hutte* 2730 m. (8,956 ft.) where I obtained a fine view of the Rimpfischhorn that brought back many memories. That day at Täsch will be remembered principally for good companionship and the repast enjoyed at the hut.

It was a strenuous excursion leaving Zermatt at 08.00 hrs. in that horrible tube train for the Sunnegga. We walked to the alpine hamlet of Tuftern where we took the path to Täsch, the same path that you would take if you decided to do the Oberrothorn climb suggested in Chapter 5. Instead of following the path right to the Oberrothorn, keep straight on the Täsch path that climbs steadily providing you with exciting views of the Weisshorn to the north west and Visptal valley with its red BVZ trains clattering to and from Brig. At one point we crossed a badly scarred area where there had been a tragic avalanche of snow and rocks only a year or so earlier which killed passengers in a taxi from Täsch. The track continues steeply until the *saddle* overlooking the Täsch Alp is reached. Helen and Hermann were in training for a visit to the Himalayas —lucky people and as they were pushing themselves they opted to descend then ascend to the Täsch Hut. How that path twisted and turned in the scorching heat so neither Hermann nor myself objected when the other wished to compose and take a photograph, what with Goats, Mountains, Glaciers and Valleys there was sufficient excuse to take a breather. What a snug haven it seemed as we first set eyes on the Täsch Hut and sank down gratefully at a vacant table to *drink* in the atmosphere of this high place. It was not only the atmosphere we drank in! we soon polished off a litre of red local wine, Rye bread, and Trockenfleich. What a memorable feast, at that moment of time, no other wine or delicacy could have tasted better. The wine was a DOLE which should be drunk at high altitude — at least this is what I have been told and I must say I am in full agreement. All of us would have liked to linger indefinitely in the sun, but that enemy of life *time* beckoned so we gathered up our belongings for the easy part — the walk back to Täsch. Before leaving we inspected a stone Madonna erected just to the south of the hut on which was a plaque explaining that it had been erected to commemorate the recent visit of the Pope to Switzerland. It had been an exacting 10 hour walk, and when we finally reached the Bahnhof Restaurant we just had time for a quick drink before the Zermatt train arrived.

66

1985
THE FURGG RIDGE (FURGGGRAT)

As much as I missed the company of Leita I must admit that I was able to set off on these long excursions without those twinges of conscience experienced so many times in the past. On this holiday, as well as the Täsch Hut excursion, I had completed the classic *Hohbalmen* trip from Zermatt via Trift-Schwarzenlager-Arben then the next day retraced familiar footsteps to the Mettelhorn summit. I still had not made a climb with Ivo and time was running out as I was only staying 9 days, so what could we do? We had climbed the Breithorn, Pollux, Rimpfischhorn, Matterhorn so what remained that, bearing my age in mind, was within my capabilities? The Strahlhorn or Allalinhorn? both of these were over 4000 m. so I doubted whether I was fit enough for such a challenge, with hind sight I must say I think I was. My ambition, ever since a friend climbed it some 40 years ago, was to climb the Wellenkuppe. I already felt selfish at having this holiday on my own so decided I must find something less expensive as the Tariff for the Wellenkuppe plus hut expenses would cost up to £180, so that fact, coupled with a weakness with my knee when descending made me abandon the idea. (Total descent to Zermatt 7,533 ft.) After a lot of discussion we decided on a traverse of the FURGGGRAT from the Kleine Matterhorn.

As we descended across the Plateau Rosa from the Cable Car station on the Kleine Matterhorn the surface was icy with skiers swooping down to Trockener Steg. The weather was perfect, to the north way down below, clouds filled the Visp Valley with the Bernese Mountains clearly visible. High above was the Testa Grigia which is the cable car station to Breuil in Italy. Within thirty minutes we approached the Theodule Pass and could see the whole of the Furgggrat from the Matterhorn to the Theodule Hut perched right by the Swiss-Italian border. The sun by now had some warmth and made the simple climb of the Theodulhorn 3468 m. (11,378 ft.) very enjoyable.

As we walked along the ridge in deep snow I felt pleased that the only snow ridge to be seen from Zermatt had yielded up its secrets after 40 years!

We reached the FURGGHORN just before noon but before we could reach its rocky base Ivo had to cut steps across the steep icy slope, and I had to move very carefully. Once off the ice we had to squeeze up a short narrow rock chimney that led to the summit where we joined two Swiss climbers and their guide for lunch. As the guide was wearing dark glasses I did not recognise him, but I discovered later he was one of the guides who, way back in 1979, excused himself from taking me up the Matterhorn.

We stayed about half an hour on top of the Furgghorn eating our lunch and watching through binoculars climbers descending the Hornli ridge of the Matterhorn. I have to admit I watched with feelings of appreciation and apprehension.

Within 10 minutes after leaving the Furgghorn, the rough track leads to a

Ivo Perren and myself on summit of Breithorn. Matterhorn in background.

Täsch hut. Weisshorn in background.

rocky outcrop with a particularly tricky pitch climbed by Ivo without a lot of difficulty. I was expected to follow but found I was unable to get over a slight overhang without the assistance of Ivo but my pride would not permit this. Just as I was beginning to think we were in the classic *catch 22* situation i.e. I would not go up and obviously Ivo did not intend to come down, he suggested I descend a few feet to a ledge and take a couple of steps round a corner to where there was a simple step and handhold up to him! Now we were approaching the end of the ridge but before we left that desolate spot I marvelled at those brave men who as prisoners of war in tattered clothing, often without adequate boots, and half-starved, managed to drag themselves over the Theodule Pass to freedom in Switzerland. Many died of exhaustion, some fell into crevasses and were killed but all were incredibly brave.

To get off the ridge we scrambled down a steep track barely visible to the Theodule Glacier. Just when I thought we were almost home and dry, the strong wind whipped my hat off never to be seen again. Over the years I have lost walking sticks and hats all over the Valais Alps....Leita just despairs. I was mistaken in thinking we were home and dry since the walk off the glacier took over 1½ hours and seemed harder than any section of the ridge. The rough morraine with massive piles of rocks and silt in never ending mounds and 15 foot waves piled on top of filthy crevassed ice. All this battered my legs and feet to sap a lot of my energy.

We reached Zermatt about 16.30 hrs. having taken the cable car from the Schwarzsee, and my first task on entering my apartment was to take a hot bath. It was sheer bliss to just lie and soak with a cold glass of lager balanced on that toilet seat! The evening was spent with Ivo and Hermine who kindly entertained me with a traditional cheese fondue, finishing with a raspberry flan, coffee and Williams liquer (43% volume — whisky is 40%!). Certainly a wonderful day I will not forget.

1986 — 1988
THE BREITHORN VIA THE EAST SADDLE

I was unable to visit Switzerland in 1986 or 1987 but in 1986 I managed two enjoyable scrambles in the Lake District. I climbed Scafell via LORDS RAKE at the same time enjoying a stay at Low Wood Hall Hotel, Nether Wasdale. The second climb, or scramble was up Pavey Ark via JACKS RAKE when I stayed at Skelwith Bridge Hotel, Ambleside. I am sorry to say that 1987 will always be remembered as the year I fell off the ladder — my friends knowing my interest in climbing were somewhat unsympathetic. As I explained I would not have fallen if I had been held on a tight rope! Fortunately I did not break a limb but my bruised side and chest are a constant reminder of my carelessness.

1988 was a special year as the whole family including Leita spent 12 days at the end of August in Zermatt and this was about my 20th visit. During this holiday our daughter Pat and our son-in-law Rod announced we were to be Grandparents for the first time. Theodora was born on 8.4.89 I do hope I can introduce her to the wonders of the Valais Alps. This news meant that Pat and Rod had their plans for summer skiing cramped, however this did mean more companionship for Leita so Ivo and I were able to plan another climb, and we decided to climb the Breithorn by the east ridge and descend by the popular west ridge.

On 31.8.88 I set off at 07.00 hrs. to meet Ivo at the cable car station. On my way I mused that 8 years ago to the day I met Ivo at the same place for our journey up to the Hornli Hut for our Matterhorn climb.

As we waited for the cable car to leave, the Matterhorn reflected a very diluted sunrise, indeed the weather looked so doubtful that Ivo, knowing what a keen photographer I am, volunteered to cancel the climb. As the cable car gained height above Furgg it was buffeted by such strong winds that the car had great difficulty in docking.

As we left the protection of the station tunnel, we felt the freezing wind but I was well clothed, wearing a woollen winter vest, thick cotton shirt, pullover, ear muffs and wollen mittens so I enjoyed the trek across the Breithorn Plateau to the mountain base. It is here that most climbers pause to put on their crampons and continue up the west ridge. We had left behind the skiers in their colourful ski suits to enjoy Europe's highest winter and summer ski field which even in summer covers 14 square miles. The weather had improved and the view of the French Alps was so clear that Mont Blanc seemed as if it was in the next valley. To the south in Italy the snow capped Gran Paradiso was clearly visible.

The interesting part of the climb was ahead as we climbed steadily up and across the south face of the Breithorn to the east ridge. The snow surface was frozen and I was able to keep pace and place my crampons in Ivo's footsteps —I was enjoying myself — this was life and I gave a silent prayer of thanks that

70

I was able to experience such a moment. I am afraid I did not time our ascent but I think it took about fifty minutes to reach the saddle ridge possibly less. About 15 minutes below the ridge I felt the effect of the altitude and had to pause a couple of minutes on two occasions in order to regain my breath. On the whole I was pleased with my fitness considering I was now 65 and had not climbed high for three years.

It was most impressive looking straight down on to the Breithorn Glacier and across to the Gorner Glacier. There was a strong cross wind that discouraged me from copying Ivo doing a balancing act on top of the narrow ridge to our left leading to the summit. As we climbed, I dropped down a couple of feet and contemplated what heroic action I would take if Ivo was blown on to the glacier below! Within 15 minutes we were on the summit 4164m (13,661 ft.). Visibility was still good much better than in 1980 but as before there were about 6 other Austrian and Italian climbers who spoilt the solitude. After photographing a 360 degree panorama, we descended quickly by the west ridge and joined the sight-seers on the Kleine Matterhorn.

1989 — 1992
ATTEMPTED ASCENT OF THE WELLENKUPPE

1989 was taken up preparing the manuscript for this book. My next visit to Zermatt was a few days in March 1990 on a marketing exercise, followed in June by a visit with Leita to take the first consignment of *Matterhorn Vision*. There was insufficient time to arrange a serious climb but we did enjoy some energetic walks and renewed our friendship with Ivo and Hermine.

1991 was an eventful year in a number of ways. Our second grand-daughter Eleanor Cantelli was born in February and already 'Ella' shows an aptitude for climbing into hair raising situations. With marketing the book and visiting friends and family there was little time for fell walking. However I did spend a great weekend at 'The Heights' in Llanberis with Dr. Peter Stevenson an ebullient young friend whose mission was to ensure I completed the Snowdon Circuit in a respectable time. The weather was very warm and the forbidden swim in our birthday suits at the finish was sheer bliss. Honestly we had no idea it was a reservoir!

My performance on Snowdon gave me an exaggerated opinion of my fitness and sowed the idea that I should obtain a further 'Leave Ticket' and tackle the Wellenkuppe with Ivo. So this was how I found myself on Thursday 20th August 1992, setting off at 1 p.m. from the Admiral Hotel, Zermatt for the Rothorn Hut. The previous day I had walked from the Schwarzsee to the Belvedere Hut (Ascent 678m — 2224ft.) in 1 hour 45 minutes, but this only lulled me still further into a false sense of achievement. Climbing from Zermatt to the Rothorn Hut (Ascent 1580m — 5183ft.) is quite another matter.

It was arranged that Ivo would meet me at the Trift Hotel (Ascent 717m — 2352ft.) at 3 p.m. I got there in under 2 hours, wearing my heavy Fitzroy climbing boots which, although ideal for glacier walking and high altitude climbing are not meant for back packing. I should have used lighter footwear to the hut.

We left Trift Hotel at 3.20 p.m. The sign post indicated a 2½ hour climb, but fortunately I had no idea of the effort that would be required. As my E.T.A. was 6.30 p.m. I was disappointed that I could see no end to the zig zags up the Moraine of the Trift Glacier. It was then 6 p.m. and I was tiring quickly. After another 30 minutes Ivo pointed out the Rothorn Hut and at my suggestion, went ahead. It was 7.15 p.m. when I thankfully entered the gloomy entrance to the hut. A wooden staircase led me to the dining room and kitchen where I found Ivo. I signed the register and was told that Ivo had reserved our bunks in one of the three dormitories on the 2nd floor.

After dinner we retired at about 8.30 p.m. The dormitory had some 20 or so mattresses raised up a couple of feet from the floor, with ours well placed nearest the door, at the entrance. How I inwardly cursed two British climbers who were the last to enter flashing their lights, talking, banging, rustling, with complete disregard for those trying to sleep. When finally the noise subsided I clapped my hands in appreciation. I hope they got the message.

At 3.30 a.m. I heard a dynamo start and shortly afterwards the Warden turned the lights on. Most of the climbers were climbing the Rothorn so we let them depart before getting dressed ourselves. Unfortunately the Warden turned the bedroom lights off. In the dark I made damn sure my pants were this time not back to front!

Outside the glacier was lit dimly by a half moon. Oh! let me utter a warning re the 'bogs' outside. Behind two 'stable' type doors (the top opens to save suffocation) were the usual wooden seats with a bung over the hole dropping to the glacier. I found that the strong upward draught made it impossible to dispose of the soiled paper which blew back on to my back side. With 'Hind Sight' most amusing!

After the adventures in the W.C. we set off at 4.30 a.m. immediately encountering many crevasses of varying size. Our way was up the Trift Glacier until we reached the steepest section where we fitted crampons prior to swinging left (South) towards the rocky base of the Wellenkuppe. By now the sky was lighter, but I was not going well because my six day visit gave me insufficient time to become acclimatized and fit. Yes, I had ignored my own advice! However I did have sufficient sense to realise I was straining myself so suggested to Ivo that we should turn back.

It was now 06.40 and we were off the glacier on to rock. *You will go better on rock* said Ivo so on we climbed. Well I did not go much better so I again suggested we should return. *If we reach that buttress*, said Ivo pointing to a protruding mass of rock some 150 feet higher, *We will see the summit*. Thus encouraged I set off again until the elusive summit could be seen. According to Ivo we were about 3780m high which meant we had just 123m (403ft.) to climb. I must say the snow summit looked further than 123m away and at the rate I was climbing it would have taken me well over an hour to reach. I did not feel sick but my legs were leaden. My brain was ticking like a computer but I could not balance how I felt with the thought of the long descent to Zermatt. Sure I could have got there (I think!) but a second night at the hut would have been necessary, and this did not appeal to me.

I was very pleased we had persevered and reached the impressive view point overlooking the 'Mittler' and 'Unter' Gabelhorn ridges, lit by the early morning sun with the Matterhorn in the background. The time was 07.30 and for a minute I was choked as I asked myself, *Why turn back with the summit so near?* This time I could not blame the weather or an accident. It was just the fear of damaging my health, plus a promise to Leita that I would not overdo things. I was no longer 57 but 69 plus.

The descent via a different route was most enjoyable with good rock, exposed pitches and wonderful views! I treasured every minute. We soon reached the edge of the Trift Glacier where we ate a little food. Crampons were refixed, and we retraced our footsteps down the glacier finding the snow had been softened considerably by the heat of the sun. The Wellenkuppe may be considered a benign mountain but the Trift Glacier demands respect not just because of the numerous concealed crevasses, but because of falling blocks of ice, loosened by the heat from the sun. The temptation is to stop and photograph the huge crumbling ice cliffs but Ivo ensured the photographs were taken from a safer position.

We called at the Hut to pick up a few possessions then descended quickly to the Trift Hotel where I bade farewell to Ivo as I wished to return to Zermatt in my own time.

I will not dwell on the after effects of the climb, sufficient to say my prudence was warranted. One day I know I will be unable to reach the high places, but it will be a sad day if I ever admit it.

Although I have once more reached the end of my story I have included two further chapters covering costs and clothing etc..

Speaking metaphorically I hope you stayed with me all the way. If you think to yourself, *well if he can do it then so can I* my literary effort will have been worthwhile — especially if you become a 'Matterhorn Climber'!

CHAPTER 9
COMPARATIVE COSTS

Due to inflation and a fluctuating currency exchange rate I realise that the figures quoted in this chapter need to be revised frequently, however it is interesting to compare the cost of financing a visit to Switzerland when travelling with a Travel Company against the cost of private travel. Whatever the rate of inflation etc., I feel that cost wise, advantages of one method of travel and accommodation over another will, when considered as a percentage of each other, remain more or less constant.

Alternative 1.
INCLUSIVE PACKAGE HOLIDAY
WITH AIR TRAVEL & HALF-BOARD

The prices of package holidays, including half fare Travel Card, vary considerably according to the Company you choose, time of year and the class of hotel.

The cost for the most popular period say 11th July — 2nd September 1993 in a three star hotel for one person is:-

7 days	Min. £431	Max. £515
14 days	Min. £694	Max. £849

These prices are for rooms with private bath/shower and w.c. The expensive rooms would be larger with a view of the Matterhorn and a balcony.

Cheaper accommodation is available for rooms without a private bath, but you may have to pay for each bath taken.

Picnic lunches costing 10 Fcs. can be made for two from fresh rolls and various fillings.

For each alternative financial package I will give a summary of the major costs for two people. Minimum figures quoted:

Suggested Cable Car Trips (Using Swiss Card 1992)

Zermatt- Schwarzsee return	Fcs. 18-50
Zermatt-Kl. Matterhorn return	Fcs. 35-00
Zermatt-Riffelberg single	Fcs. 17-40
	Fcs. 70-90

Estimated 14 Day package for two 1993:-

Flight & accommodation	£1388
12 days picnic lunches	56
Extra cable car rides using	66
Swiss Card (£1 = Fcs. 2-14)	
Check current exchange rate	
	£1510

Alternative 2.

INDEPENDENT TRAVEL WITH HALF-BOARD
ACCOMMODATION IN A TWO STAR HOTEL

Flight Costs:

The present economic difficulties make it imperative for most of us to seek the best value for money. As schedule flights by Swiss Air and British Airways have been priced above what I am prepared to pay I will quote below an air fare from the 'Earlybird Edition' of Summer 1993 Falcon Flights a company I have used on several occasions.

Return Flight Gatwick to Zurich or Geneva 1.7.93 — 5.9.93

Cost £139 Return

Flights from Manchester to Geneva only 1.7.93 — 5.9.93

Cost £179 Return

Swiss Train Fare Costs:

The most economical ticket is a 'Transfer Ticket' costing £35 providing a return journey from Geneva (or any Swiss Airport) to Zermatt.

OR

A 'Swiss Card' valid for one month costing £50 as from 1.1.93. This gives greater flexibility allowing one day transfers from frontier stations or airports to your destination in Switzerland and back PLUS 50% reductions for additional rail excursions. It is comforting to have this ticket if the weather is very wet since you would save £12 per person on a return ticket Zermatt to Brig. Reductions are also available with the Swiss Card on Cable Car fares e.g. a further £8 would be saved in total on return fares to the Schwarzsee and Klein Matterhorn.

HOTEL (TWO STAR) ACCOMMODATION
WITH HALF-BOARD & PRIVATE FACILITIES

Cost per person 77 Fcs. — 100 Fcs. per day
At an Exchange Rate of £1 = Fcs. 2-14
Then 7 nights cost between £251 and £327

Estimated independent travel costs for two over 14 days (1993)

	£
Charter Flights — £139 x 2	278
Swiss Travel Card — £50 x 2	100
Cable Car costs (See Alternative 1.)	66
Minimum cost for 14 nights — £502 x 2	1004
Estimated 12 days Picnic Lunches	56
	1504

Note: 3 Star Hotel would cost from £52 to £261 extra per person over 14 nights.

Alternative 3.

PRIVATE ACCOMMODATION IN 2 BED APARTMENT PLUS TRAVEL (1992)

Travel costs as specified in alternative 2.	£ 378
Cost of apartment for 2 for two weeks = Fcs 840 (Converted at 2.14 Fcs to £1)	£ 392
Estimated cost of food for two weeks — Fcs 360 at 2.14	£ 168
Cable car fares (Swiss Card) for two	66
Local Tax at Fcs 1.80 per day per person = Fcs 50.40 (Converted at Fcs 2.14 to £1) approx.	23

Note: Local taxes are used to improve and maintain footpaths, and other tourist amenities. Hotel costs are inclusive of this tax.

TOTAL MAJOR COSTS	£1027

ESTIMATED GUIDE'S FEES FROM (1992)

RIFFELHORN —	Practice climb	300.00 Fcs
	Train Fare — return Guide	19.50 Fcs
	Train Fare — single, self	12.00 Fcs
BREITHORN —	Acclimatization climb	
	Daily guided party fee	110.00 Fcs
	Return Fare — Kleine M'horn	35.00 Fcs
MATTERHORN —	Hörnligrat	610.00 Fcs
	Return Fare — Schwarzsee	18.50 Fcs
	Est. overnight costs for self and Guide	140.00 Fcs
	Subscription to Schweizerische Rettungsflugwacht (unless your Insurance Cover provides for rescue costs)	30.00 Fcs
		1275.00 Fcs

Sterling equivalent when converted at Fcs 2.14 to £1	=	£595	
at Fcs 1.46 to $1 U.S	=	$873 U.S.	

Fares have been calculated assuming the use of a Swiss Card

All figures quoted are to the nearest £ or Franc and given for guidance only.

An up to date tariff, showing fees for all guided ascents from Zermatt can be obtained from the Guides' Office. Do read and understand the general conditions and rules printed in English, French and German (copy printed in Glossary) on the back of the tariff.

Although the fees seem formidable, I can assure you that we *Beginners* receive value for money. Remember our lives are literally in the hands of our guide. You have only to slip once, as indeed I did, and your fall is immediately arrested by the tight belay the guide has on you. Believe me if this happens you would feel that if you could afford it, you would pay double. What is your life worth to you and your family.

The Guide's tariff is value for money particularly when you consider the discomfort of staying in mountain huts with few modern conveniences, rising between 03.00 hrs. and 04.00 hrs. and battling with the elements — not to mention ourselves. For once I agree with F. S. Smythe that the Guides earn *every centime of their pay*, but this is their chosen profession and I do not accept that we *Tourists* have a debilitating, even souring effect on the Alpine Guide.

Remember we hope there will be the supreme thrill and satisfaction of standing on the summit of the Matterhorn BUT, unless you accept that your ambition can only be achieved at a physical and financial cost then I say — think twice, and perhaps stay on the hills.

The total cost of your holiday plus climbing costs is considerable, and not everybody is fortunate enough to have so much surplus capital. However these days, provided you have a surplus of income over current expenditure, banks will fund your holiday.

I do feel that the figures mentioned in this chapter are likely to discourage would be Matterhorn Climbers. However substantial economies in travel and accommodation costs can be made by fit young folk willing to 'rough it'.

There are approximately 250 Walking/Mountaineering Clubs in the U.K. affiliated to the B.M.C., one of these clubs is the Bridlington Walking and Climbing Club. In 1992 three members shared the expense of a camping holiday at Chamonix. All three had previous Alpine climbing experience and successfully completed, without guides, the ascent of Mont Blanc at a fraction of the costs quoted above.

As the Matterhorn poses different hazards from Mont Blanc only experienced Alpine Rock Climbers should attempt the Matterhorn without guides.

Each year the B.M.C. produces for members a booklet listing numerous mountaineering courses arranged by themselves, or by guides and instructors holding appropriate, nationally-recognised qualifications. Some of these courses include an ascent of the Matterhorn so are worth considering from a practical and financial point of view.

CHAPTER 10

CLOTHING ETC.

I feel that I cannot do better than to quote verbatum from a leaflet, issued by the Zermatt Guides' Office, giving advice on climbing the Matterhorn.

"Your clothes for this lofty adventure should include good leather mountain boots with rubber soles which can be rented at Zermatt, warm socks and stockings, climbing trousers or knickerbockers, warm woollen longsleeved underwear which absorbs perspiration and dries quickly, sport shirt, sweater, a windbreaker, two pairs of woollen gloves, head protection, preferably two pairs of sunglasses, suntan lotion and cream for your lips."

I personally do not like the idea of hiring mountain boots for two reasons. Firstly if you hire boots then the inference must be that the climb is to be a *one off job* and I cannot respect a mentality that permits such an attitude. Secondly how can a hired pair of boots be comfortable? Assuming you have no boots, why not buy a good pair?

It is most important that your boots are the correct length. When buying boots always take with you the socks you will wear for climbing. A good retailer will measure your foot and the inside of the boot to check that there is sufficient room. Walking down, down, down, jams your big toe into the boot. There must be sufficient room to wiggle your toes in comfort!

Since 1978 I have been satisfied with a pair of leather boots from the Italian Manufacturer SCARPA that have doubled up as walking as well as climbing boots. These boots were made in the traditional manner having a sewn welt with a midsole containing a stiffener that enabled flexible crampons to be worn.

Today you find quality leather mountaineering boots with uppers made of leather, tanned in such a way as to improve their waterproofing qualities. In addition the strength and waterproofing of the boot has been improved by using a stitched and bonded type of construction. Scarpa are making a boot called 'Scarpa Fitzroy' marketed by Berghaus who emphasise the following advantages:-

    1. The rubber rand and midsole are stiffened by a light aluminium plate, and is constructed by the bonding and *Blake* sewn method as a one-piece unit.

    2. The one-piece unit permits the use of modern style clip-on crampons.

    3. Either articulated or rigid crampons can be worn.

I prefer manufacturers who use more hooks and fewer D rings on their boots, as I find it difficult to maintain the tension on the lace when threading the lace through the D rings.

Ideally, finances permitting, it is preferable to have a pair of boots for walking and another pair for climbing since a boot containing a stiffener is heavier than a more flexible boot just intended for walking. I do now possess a Scarpa Alp Attak pair of walking boots with a *Performance Flex* midsole which is lighter than my climbing boot, yet gives my weak ankles the desired support.

I give below a list of clothing I wear for my climbs. When I chose my clothing I believed that the way to keep warm was to put more on when you were cold, and to take off something if you were too hot. This idea has been proved wrong as I will mention later!

All the time manufacturers are marketing improvements to under and top clothing and boots so it is advisable to shop around before making your final choice.

SOCKS: I have put these first as I consider that climbing and walking cannot be enjoyed unless your feet are comfortable. We all have preferences, but I wear one thin pair of cotton socks, (not too thin or they can 'ruck' up) and one thick pair of socks. The thick pair are made from 70% wool and reinforced with 30% nylon, and knitted in a loop method which gives added protection to the foot from pressure points within the boot. One pressure point likely to be troublesome is the toe seam, but this can be largely avoided if you ensure that the sock is fully fashioned.

VESTS: Mine have been woollen but not long sleeved. As we all know from experience during ascents we sweat, particularly if wearing waterproof anoraks made of nylon or similar material, so unless we are careful chill rapidly when not exerting ourselves. Now tests have proved that this problem can be largely overcome by wearing a set of synthetic fibre clothing consisting of three layers. Within the constraints of any so called 'breathable fabric' it is claimed that each fibre layer draws moisture away from the body by a process that has been dubbed 'Wicking'.

The first layer is of course worn next to the skin, and allows body moisture to pass through to the second layer. Berghaus offer either a lightweight or midweight 100% Polyester shirt known as their 'Active Comfort Layer' (A.C.L.). Helly-Hansen offer a choice of four underwear garments. Three are made from 100% Polypropylene publicised as 'Lifa Super' 'Super Net' and 'Thermal', and their fourth choice is called 'Thermal Wool' which is a mixture of their Lifa Super on the inside of the fabric and wool for insulation. The manufacturers claim that 'Thermal Wool' does not cause itching.

It is recommended that the second layer of the three should be a jacket made from materials that will continue the 'wicking' process. Both of the above mentioned manufacturers in common with other manufacturers market garments compatible with this aim.

Our body moisture finally evaporates through the third (if worn) outer 'Shell' — see under 'Anorak'.

LONG PANTS/LONG JOHNS: are pure cotton which I find helps to keep out the cold but are not too hot on the descent when the temperature rises. As described above, synthetic fibres are now used to make *Long Johns* but I have not seen any report that refers to one's comfort when the temperature suddenly rises. However cotton based garments are criticised by some for retaining moisture and not retaining body heat.

ANORAK: Many climbers do not wear one, but I like to have zip pockets to hold my small camera (Rollei 35T) and film. The anorak is made of windproof and showerproof cotton, and is long enough to cover my backside — a useful factor when sitting down. However if equipping yourself for the first time, it would be prudent to consider the 3 layer recommendations in which case your outer *shell* might well be a jacket made from a fabric containing pores that permit sweat vapour to pass out without rain water soaking through. Again one must not forget the time of year one is climbing. It is just as exhausting to be too hot as it is to be too cold.

The total cost of a complete set, i.e. two inner layers and outer shell is well over £200, which may seem expensive until compared with golfing fees and the cost of golf clubs and the 19th hole. Because of the expenses and possible body temperature problems, I would proceed with caution trying out one layer at a time. Some of us are allergic to wool and others to some synthetic fibres.

CLIMBING TROUSERS: There is a wide choice. Mine are wool with reinforced seat and knee patches. I have worn ordinary thick wool trousers with gaiters.

GLOVES OR MITTENS: Thick waterproof wool is preferable. In 1980 I wore only open ended mittens thinking I would not be able to find handholes if I wore gloves or mittens. This was a silly decision, so be warned.

SHIRT: Thick cotton type.

PULLOVER: Thick wool type with sleeves. I find polo neck pullovers have a very limited opening for the head and consequently sun glasses are dislodged when the pullover is pulled over the head.

WOOL HELMET: Ideal until the sun rises. Best worn as a Balaclava tucked down your neck. I wore mine as a glorified commando hat — see chapter on climb!

SUNGLASSES: Take two pairs in case one pair gets lost or damaged. If your eyesight is good, goggles are preferred.

FOOD: Glucose sweets. Chocolate. Dried fruit — Christmas type fruit cake goes down a treat.

RUCKSACK: My own is a 'Karrimor' without a frame as this can become wedged in rock. It must be waterproof, light-weight and have waist and shoulder straps that can be adjusted quickly and easily. I find it useful if the rucksack has one or two smaller pockets in which you can carry small items you may need during the climb. As a keen photographer I prefer a red rucksack for photography and quick identification by aircraft in case of need. Prolonged rain can seep into anything so pack your things in waterproof bags.

ODDMENTS: Plasters — just in case your boots give you a blister or you accidentally cut yourself. Torch. Handkerchieves. Small towel. Hot drink in preference to cold.

This chapter does not pretend to be a comprehensive guide on mountain gear, but is simply to help you avoid some of the mistakes I made.

GLOSSARY

Belay	An anchor point round which a rope can be twisted to secure a climber.
Buttress	A mass of rock protruding from the mountain-side.
Boot stiffener	Usually a light Aluminium plate sandwiched between the upper and lower soles of a climbing boot to maintain rigidity, to assist in the use of crampons, or balancing on narrow rock ledges.
Chimney	A narrow vertical gully in rock.
Couloir	Gully or furrow in the mountain-side.
Crampon	Metal frame with spikes fitting the sole of the boot for use when crossing an icy surface.
Crevasse	A deep fissure in glacial ice.
Moraine	Accumulation of rocks and rubble carried along by glacial movement.
Pitch	A section of difficult ice or rock between ledges or belay points.
Scree	Slope of small loose stones.
Traverse	To cross a ridge or mountain slope horizontally.

USEFUL ADDRESSES

SWISS NATIONAL TOURIST OFFICES:-

United Kingdom	Swiss Centre New Coventry Street London W1V 8EE	Tel: (071) 734-1921
Australia/New Zealand	P.O. Box 82 Edgecliff Sydney, NSW 2027	Tel: 02-3261799
Canada	154 University Avenue Toronto Ontario M5H 3Z4	Tel: (416) 868-0584
Japan	Tokyo 107 C.S. Tower 2nd Floor 1-11-30 Akasaka Minato-ku	Tel: 03/589 5588
USA	608 Fifth Avenue New York NY 10020	Tel: (212) 757-5944
	260 Stockton Street San Francisco CA 94108	Tel: (415) 362-2260

150 New Michigan Avenue
Chicago 1L 60601   Tel: (312) 630-5840

MOUNTAIN GUIDE OFFICE ZERMATT
Bergführrerburo
CH-3920 Zermatt   Tel: 028/67 34 56

HELIPORT ZERMATT
Air Zermatt SA
3920 Zermatt
Heliport   Tel: 028/67 34 87 (08.00-17.30 hrs.)

BRITISH ASSOCIATION OF MOUNTAIN GUIDES
B.M.C.
Crawford House
Precinct Centre
Booth Street East
Manchester M13 9RZ
England   Tel: (061) 274-3264

BMC INSURANCE MANAGER
British Mountaineering Council
Crawford House
Precinct Centre
Booth Street East
Manchester M13 9RZ
England   Tel: (061) 273-5835

MOUNTAIN CLOTHING AND EQUIPMENT ADDRESSES

HELLEY-HANSEN (UK) LTD. — Clothing
College street
Kempston
Bedford
Bedfordshire
MK42 8NA
England   Tel: (0234) 266966

BERGHAUS LIMITED — Clothing, Boots, Ice Axes,
Rucksacks Gaiters.
34 Dean Street
Newcastle upon Tyne
NE1 1PG   Tel: (091) 415 0200

KARRIMOR INTERNATIONAL LTD — Clothing
Rucksacks, & Equipment.
Petrey Road
Clayton-Le-Moors
Accrington
Lancashire
BB5 5JP   Tel: (0254) 385911

In most towns and cities specialist walking and climbing shops can give advice and name other good manufacturers.

MOUNTAIN GUIDES' FEES FROM 1992

Auskünfte und Anmeldung:
Bergführerbüro 3920 Zermatt
Telefon (028) 67 34 56

Balfrin	350.-
Ulrichshorn	350.-
Nadelhorn-Ulrichshorn von Bordier	450.-
* Südlenz mit Abstieg nach Randa	490.-
Stecknadelhorn	420.-
Dürrenhorn	460.-
Hohberghorn	460.-
Stecknadelhorn-Nadelhorn mit Abstieg nach Saas-Fee	540.-
* Südlenz und Nadelhorn mit Abstieg nach Saas-Fee	570.-
* Dom über Festigrat	610.-
- über Hohberggletscher	610.-
* Hohberghorn-Stecknadelhorn-Nadelhorn	550.-
* Dieselben Gipfel mit Ulrichshorn	620.-
Südlenz bis und mit Hohberghorn	NV
- bis und mit Dürrenhorn	NV
Mischabelbiwak	430.-
* Täschhorn ab Domhütte	610.-
- über den Grat zum Dom	NV
* - ab Täschhütte	680.-
* - ab Mischabelbiwak	550.-
- Teufelsgrat	NV
Übergänge nach Saas-Fee	430.-
* Leiterspitzen	420.-
Alphubel Normalroute	410.-
- Eisnase	430.-
* - Rotgrat	580.-
- Traversierung über Mischabeljoch	490.-
* - Westgrat	660.-
* - Westrippe	720.-
- mit Abstieg nach Saas-Fee	430.-
Allalinhorn mit Feekopf	490.-
- und Abstieg nach Saas-Fee	520.-
* Südgrat über Feekopf und zurück	550.-
Feekopf	370.-
Rimpfischhorn ab Täschhütte	470.-
- ab Fluhalp	470.-
* - Nord-Grat	560.-
* - West-Flanke	560.-
- mit Abstieg nach Saas-Fee	500.-
Strahlhorn ab Fluhalp	470.-
- von Schwarzberg-Weisstor	480.-
- mit Abstieg nach Saas-Fee	470.-
- Alderspitze	410.-
Cima di Jazzi	340.-
Fillarhorn	340.-
Jägerhorn	430.-

Monte Rosa Nordend	570.-
- Catharinagrat	NV
* - Morshead Sporn	590.-
* Monte Rosa Dufourspitze	610.-
* - vom Silbersattel	620.-
* - über Cresta Rey	680.-
* - Traversierung über Zumsteinspitze- ab Monte-Rosa Hütte	720.-
* - Traversierung über Zumsteinspitze ab Margherita	570.-
- Ost-Wand (Marinelli)	NV
Zumsteinspitze	450.-
Parrotspitze	430.-
Signalkuppe	550.-
Ludwigshöne	430.-
Schwarzhorn	430.-
Vincents-Pyramide	430.-
Parrotspitze-Ludwigshöhe Schwarzhorn-Vincentspyramide ab Monte Rosa Hütte	720.-
- ab Margherita o. Gnifetti	640.-
* Lyskamm ab Monte Rosa Hütte	550.-
* - ab Margherita o. Gnifetti	450.-
* - Traversierung ab Monte Rosa Hütte	620.-
* - Traversierung ab Margherita/Gnifetti/Sella oder umgekehrt	520.-
Traversierung ab Sella zur Signalkuppe	600.-
- Nord-Wand	NV
* Lyskamm-Castor ab Margherita/Gnifetti/Klein Matterhorn oder umgekehrt	610.
* ab Monte Rosa Hütte	720.-
Castor-Lyskamm-Signalkuppe ab Klein Matterhorn	800.-
Castor-Lyskamm-Gnifetti ab Klein Matterhorn	700.-
Castor-Lyskamm ab Klein Matterhorn und zurück	650.-
* Lyskamm-Castor-Pollux - ab Margherita/Gnifetti/Klein Matterhorn oder umgekehrt	750.-
* ab Monte Rosa Hütte	850.-
Castor-Pollux ab Klein Matterhorn oder Sellahütte	550.-
Castor ab Klein Matterhorn oder Sellahütte	410.-
- ab Monte Rosa Hütte	490.-
Pollux ab Klein Matterhorn	400.-
Breithorn ab Klein Matterhorn	300.-
- ab Gandegghütte	430.-

- klassische Route Westseite 440.-
- direkte Nordwestwand
  (Welzenbach)................................. NV
* - Triftjegrat 640.-
- Younggrat .... NV
* - Traversierung 610.-
- halbe Traversierung 430.-
- vom Schwarztor ganger Grat .... NV
Klein Matterhorn
* Nordwestgrat 400.-
Theodulhorn 350.-
- und Furggrat................................ 400.-
Riffelhorn
zwei mittelschwere Aufstiege 300.-
* - Thermometer, Kante oder
  Groganloch................................. 340.-
* - Matterhorncouloir 400.-
Matterhorn Hörnligrat........................ 610.-
- Traversierung
- Hörnli-Italienergrat....................... 770.-
- Zmuttgrat 770.-
- Traversierung
Zmutt-Italienergrat .... NV
- Furggengrat................................ NV
* Dent-d'Hérens Normalroute 600.-
- Ostgrat..................................... NV
Tête Blanche Normalroute 390.-
- mit Abstieg in ein Nachbartal 460.-
Tête de Valpeline............................ 390.-
* Wandfluhhorn Süd Pfeiler................. 720.-
* Dent Blanche Normalroute 650.-
- Viereselsgrat .... NV
- Ferpèclegrat............................... NV
Pointe de Zinal
- ab Schönbülhütte 430.-
* - Südostgrat 470.-
Mont Durand (Arbenhorn)................. 340.-
Aebihorn 340.-
Aebihorn und Pointe de Zinal
vom Arbenbiwak............................. 480.-

* Ober-Gabelhorn
  über Wellenkuppe 570.-
* - Arbgrat vom Arbenbiwak 640.-
* - Traversierung 700.-
* - Sud-Wand .... NV
* - Südostgrat vom Arbenbiwak 730.-
- Nordwand ab Rothornhütte .... NV
Unter-Gabelhorn............................. 430.-
Wellenkuppe 410.-
* Trifthorn 440.-
* Zinalrothorn Normalroute 500.-
* - Traversierung nach Mountet............ 560.-
* - Rothorngrat............................... 590.-
* - von Triftjoch über Trifthorn 640.-
* - Kanzelgrat 620.-
- Ostwand .... NV
* Ober Mominghorn
  ab Rothornhütte............................ 460.-
- und Zinalrothorn .... NV
Aeschihorn.................................. 340.-
Schalihorn ab Rothornhütte................ 490.-
- ab Weisshornhütte 470.-
* Weisshorn Normalroute 650.-
- Schaligrat.................................. NV
* - Nordgrat.................................. 740.-
- Traversierung .... NV
Bishorn von Topalihütte 510.-
Brunegghorn 420.-
* Brunegghorn Wand......................... 560.-

Hüttentarife
Rothorn-, Schönbühl-, Dom-
und Weisshornhütte............................ 170.-
Monte Rosa-, Matterhorn-
und Täschhütte................................ 140.-
Fluhalp und Gandegg........................... 120.-
Arbenbiwak 300.-

Sämtliche Preise in Schweizer Franken.

SAC-Hüttentaxen	**Taxes dans les cabanes**	**CAS/SAC Hut Charges**
(unverbindlich)	(sans garantie)	(without engagement)
	Halbpension	
	Demi-pension	ca. Fr. 45.-
	Half-pension	

General conditions and rules

1. Each guided climb or tour not mentioned in this tariff is subject to a preliminary special arrangement between the guide and his client, based on a daily rate of Sfrs. 300.-. The tours marked NV remain reserved.

2. If more than 2 persons share the services of one guide, the fees quoted in this list may be increased by 10% for each additional person (maximum 50%). This refers to tours according to tariff. It is the duty of the guide to limit the number of participants in accordance with the degree of difficulty of the envisaged climb or tour.

3. Should two or more summits (not mentioned in the tariff) be climbed in one day special arrangements with the guide must be made in advance.

4. Board and accommodation of the guide in huts and mountain hotels, the cost of food consumed by the guide on tours, as well as his travelling expenses are chargeable to his client(s).

5. If the guide, on completion of a mountain crossing or crossing of a mountain pass, needs an additional day for his journey home, he is entitled to an extra payment of Sfrs. 300.- plus his travel expenses.

6. In the event of any engagement covering a period of more than 3 days, the daily allowance payable to the guide amounts to a minimum of Sfrs. 300.-. For each ascent 30% of the tariff is being charged.

7. The charge for a day spent waiting in the hut due to bad weather is fixed at Sfrs. 300.-.

8. The ascent to a hut is usually included in the guides fee.

9. Appropriate legal action shall be taken in call cases of infringements or contraventions of the above rules and non-observance of the stipulated rates. Appeals from any complaints made by the competent authorities in this connection may be filed with the Council of State within 20 days from the date of publication of said complaint.

10. A client who, for any reason whatsoever, is obliged to cancel an engagement, will be charged 50% of the agreed fee.

11. All skitours not mentioned in the tariff and reached by all means of transportation are chargeable with Sfrs. 300.-.

12. If the starting point of a tour is reached by helicopter, the transport cost for the guide will be deduced from the tariff.

13. For the climbs marked with a star, the guide has the right to ask for an additional 20% if more than one person is taken.

14. For safety reasons a guide will only take one person at a time up the Matterhorn.

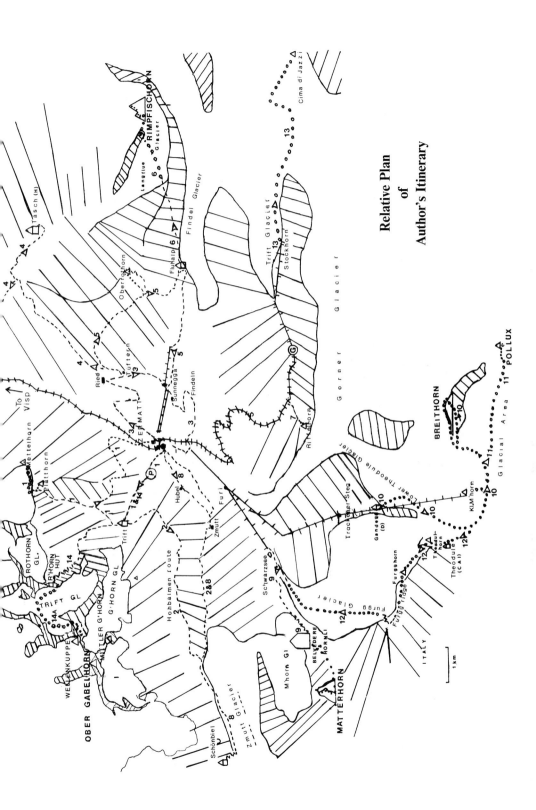

Relative Plan
of
Author's Itinerary

1 km

KEY

Alpine and rocky terrain

Foot trail   - - - - - - -

Snow/Glacial walking and climbing   ○ ○ ○ ○ ○ ○

Rock climbing   ● ● ●

Mountain Huts (All provide refreshments during season)

Pension Eidelweiss   (P)   Gornergrat Hotel   (G)

Railways   ┼┼┼┼┼┼┤

Cable car lift   ┴┴┴┴┴

Sunnega Alpen Metro   ▭▭▭▭▭

Walks and climbs from — Zermatt.

1.   Trift — Platthorn — Mettelhorn and return (Very strenuous).

2.   Circular route — Trift — Hohbalmen and return on lower path to Zmutt and Zermatt (Strenuous).

3.   Circular walk — Reid — Tuftern — Sunnegga — Findeln — Zermatt.

4.   Commencing Zermatt or Sunnegga via Tuftern — Tasch Hut — Tasch and return by train. (Strenuous).

5.   Tuftern — Oberrothorn — Fluhalp — Sunnegga (Very strenuous).

6.   Fluhalp — Rimpfischhorn (Climb).

7.   Riffelhorn (Climb).

8.   Hubel — Zmutt — Schonbiel Hut and return (Strenuous).

9.   Schwarzsee — Hornli & Belvedere huts and Matterhorn climb if you are lucky. Walk to huts very strenuous unless cable lift used.

10.   Gandegg Hut — Kl. Matterhorn-Breithorn (Climb).

11.   Kl. Matterhorn — Pollux (Climb).

12.   Kl. Matterhorn — Theodul hut — Furgghorn — Furgg ridge — Furgg Gl. — Schwarzsee. (Guided walk).

13.   Stockhorn — Cimi di Jazzi (Climb).

14.   Zermatt — Trift — Rothorn Hut (Very strenuous).

14a   Rothorn Hut — Wellenkuppe (Climb).